Healing Houses

Healing Houses

Transforming Sick Houses Into Healthy Homes

Sheldon Norberg

Ronin Publishing
Berkeley, Ca

Healing Houses
Transforming Sick Houses into Health Homes

ISBN: 978-1-57951-1807
Released simultaneously in ebook
E-ISBN: 978-57951-1968

Published by
Ronin Publishing, Inc.
PO Box 3436
Oakland, CA 94609
www.roninpub.com

Production:

Book Design: Pete Masterson, Aeonix Publishing Group
www.aeonix.com
Cover Design: Howard Penner
Text: Adobe Minion Pro, 11pt

Library of Congress Card Number: 2015932157
Distributed to the book trade by PGW/Perseus

Previously published by North Mountain Publishing
Previous ISBN: 978-0967623 1-6-0

Acknowledgments

The author would like to thank:

Mary Swanson, M.L.S.B.C. - a tremendous clairvoyant whose astrology work brought me to the path of self recognition and restoration

Francesca McCartney, Ph.D. – Founder and Director of The Academy of Intuition Medicine®, and author of *Body of Health*, who gave me the tools and training that allowed me to develop my divergent practice.
("Intuition Medicine" is a registered trademark of Francesca McCartney, Ph.D being used with permission)

Angela Wu, O.M.D. – Whose loving care, precision needling (literally and figuratively), and teachings have saved my life in more ways than one.

My Parents – whose relentless rationality trained me to prove all of this to myself.

Suzanne and our beautiful children, Gryphon and Astrid, for giving me a whole new perspective on Love.

The Sheldon Family, for being with me through all this.

Bright Moments!

The Author and Publisher would like to thank Ms. Joann Deck, formerly Senior Editor at Crossings Press, for believing in this book, her gentle and incredibly accurate correction, and her cheerful demeanor.

We also wish to thank Pete Masterson for his hard work, unerring guidance.

Dedication

This book is dedicated to *My Clients*, without whose willingness to confront the irrational, none of this could have happened.

Table of Contents

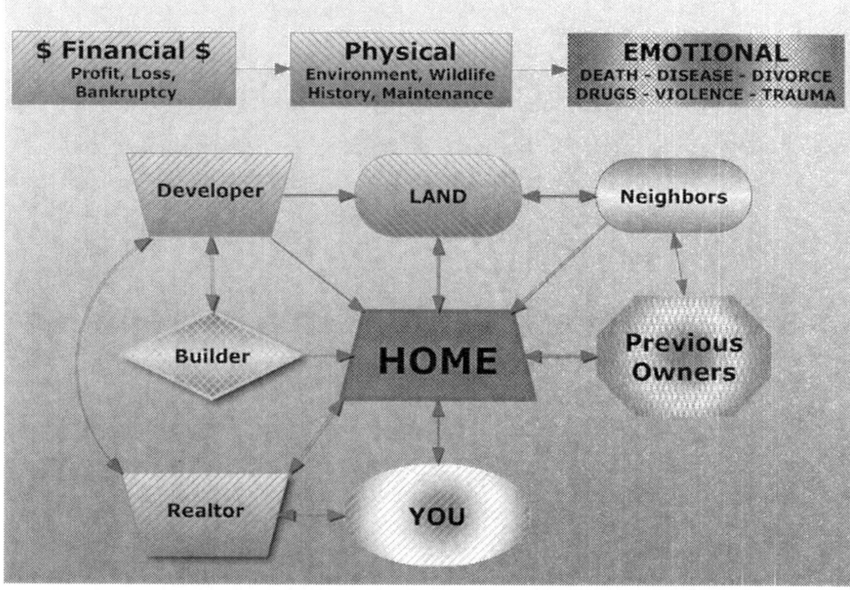

Energetic Influences Surround Your Home

The three primary Energetic Influences on a home are Physical, Financial, and Emotional. Obviously, YOU will have a great deal invested in your HOME, primarily in the Financial and Emotional categories, which will leave you open to match the vibratory energy of previous tenants along those same lines, or be unable to see where related problems may exist.

Previous Owners have a lot to do with the immediate feel of the house, and the events that can set the vibrational pattern range from death and divorce to drug use or child abuse and more. Oddly enough, even the Neighbors and their historic relationship retain some bandwidth

Land may carry the ancestral energy or trauma of native peoples, more recent wars, loss of traditional habitat or farms, as well as direct influences from birds, animals, or insects.

Developer's relationships with the Builder and Realtor also play into the house's energy, and set the initial Financial tone, although it can stem from the history that came before them.

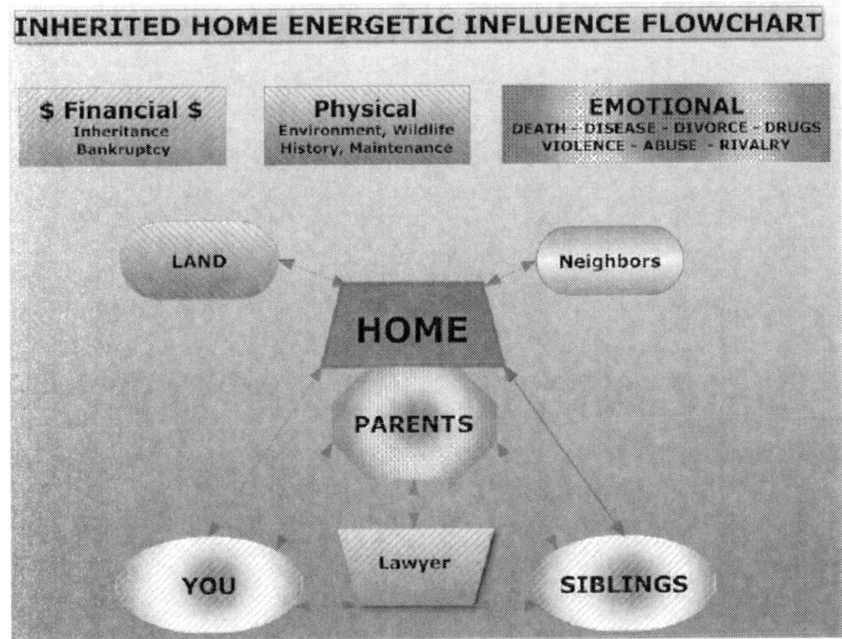

Energetic Influences in Inherited Homes

In Inherited HOMES, there are the deeply rooted aspects of your relationship to your PARENTS and SIBLINGS, your mutual histories of living in the house, and any Emotional difficulties in those relationships can turn parts of the house into major triggers. When the Financial cards come out, and the Lawyers step in, the resulting acrimony can create further external influences that need to be defused and shielded against.

Preface

HAVE YOU EVER WALKED INTO a house that just didn't *feel* right? A house that made you uncomfortable, sad perhaps, or somehow nervous? Perhaps it was a house that your friend had moved into, but which you preferred to avoid, making dates at some neutral location. Maybe your friend told you they didn't like it either, that odd things seemed to happen there; inexplicable noises, electrical and mechanical failures, uncomfortable feelings or feelings that didn't feel like *their own*. Maybe your friend didn't talk about it. Maybe you noticed them change, over time, becoming anxious, depressed, or otherwise affected in some way.

Maybe you were the person who bought that house. Did your experience pit you against your rational mind? Did you tell yourself that the things that were happening couldn't really be happening? Were you afraid to tell your friends, or family, for fear of *appearing insane?* Or did you fear for your *own* sanity? These are the kind of feelings that my clients often tell me about, when they finally call me to heal their house. *Finally,* because to call me generally means that they have tried everything, and given up on "rational" explanation.

My clients are high-functioning, serious people, from all walks of life, whose lives have been disrupted by things they would prefer to deny the existence of. Until they start to accept that rationality *includes* perceiving the interconnection between our emotional energy and matter, their experience is fighting against their belief system. They have unexpectedly come to a crossroads, simply by moving into a house. What's more, this house holds energy that is so difficult to live with that they needed my help.

If you're reading this, it's likely that you've encountered one of these houses (or live in one!) and want to understand them better. This book is an attempt to categorize and explain the different levels of phenomenon caused by misdirected and unresolved human energy. It's by no means exhaustive, I'm sure, but it spans the breadth of my 20-year-career, and I believe it presents the most lucid model of how the energetic world interacts with our emotional and physical bodies here on the physical plane, in our homes.

Why This Book?

Healing Houses was not my intended career. Nor was it my intention when I began my intuitive training. As a man (and there are certainly far fewer men than women involved in intuitive disciplines), the training that I was undertaking was something I kept pretty private. As I embarked on that path and began changing my life, I shed some of my friends and entered into a reclusive period, particularly for me. While I was developing a more grounded and clear sense of self, I didn't feel particularly secure in sharing that with my dude friends, or dealing with their likely razzings.

When I began developing the housework, I stepped beyond my personal program of self reformation and into the realm of scientific implausibility, a range of actions intended to alter the energetic substrate of physical matter. It was pretty bizarre stuff, and likely to be dismissed as crazy by most rational people, as I assumed my friends were.

As hippy-dippy as I might have been at times, I certainly tried to hold to a rational materialistic framework, and feared being derided for my beliefs as much as anyone. They weren't even *beliefs* at that point, but distinct experiences, which contradicted my own belief system. So I kept it all pretty much to myself. What I found, however, was when I did open up to someone about the work I was doing, they almost invariably had a story, from their childhood or adult life, about an experience that left an indelible impression on them. They too struggled with the fact that there is an energetic world that we are engaged in, despite our rationalistic mindset.

Their stories frequently had to do with houses: houses they grew up in, houses their grandparents lived in, houses they moved into as roommates when they left home, but also experiences they had around the deaths of relatives or friends. As I became more confident about my work, and more able to support it as a rational concept, more people were discreetly forthcoming with their stories, stories which still made them uncomfortable, because they had been told for so long to distrust *their own experience*, no matter how vivid or life changing it had been.

This book is an attempt to verify and clarify the reality of the energetic situations that we engage in simply by living in our homes, to bring awareness of this reality to others, and to offer some reassurance to those whose homes hold distinctly difficult energy. For those who have always considered that there was more to the "real" world than the physical plane, this book will be a valuable reference tool.

I did not design this book as a training manual. The work I do, as you will see, causes me to encounter some very unpleasant situations that I cannot prepare you for. I do, however, recognize the importance of presenting readers with tools for approaching their own homes, so that they can start out or finish up on the right foot. With a template for understanding the energetic construct of your house and some basic practices for tuning it up, this book will give you a clear approach to making your home feel like your own, and a clear idea of why to call me if you can't.

Part I

Houses and Energy

Does My House Need Healing?

Instructions: Relax with your eyes closed and imagine *being in* your house, moving about, doing routine activities or just hanging out. For each of the following questions, notice how you feel being in your house, then rate how the item reflects how you feel, with 1 being not at all like me, and 9 being very much like me.

Rating scale: (Not at all like me) 1 . . . . . . 9 (Very much like me)

__ 1) I feel *uncomfortable* in my house.

__ 2) I tend to *avoid* certain rooms in my house.

__ 3) My *behavior has changed* since moving into my house.

__ 4) My *sleep has been fitful* since moving into my house.

__ 5) I experience a *sense of compressed headroom* in my house.

__ 6) I experience a *sense of different pressure* in certain rooms in my house.

__ 7) Some rooms in my house have a *cold chill.*

__ 8) Some rooms in my house have an *inexplicable smell.*

__ 9) There are frequent *electrical and telephone disruptions* in my house.

__ 10) I have *sensed ghosts* in my house.

Healing Need: Add up the rating for each item.

70-90: **Urgent Need**: Your house is exhibiting high energetic influence from many sourses and is in urgent need of psychic house cleaning.

40-60: **Moderate Need:** Your house is exhibiting some energetic influences from some sources and could benefit from psychic house cleaning.

10-30: **Low Need:** Your house is exhibiting low energetic influences from few sources and is not in need of psychic house cleaning.

Basics

ENERGY FOLLOWS YOUR THOUGHT. SIMPLE as that. We transmit and receive energy signals constantly. Our thoughts transmit energy, our emotions transmit energy, our actions transmit energy. We are in constant energetic communication with each other. Usually projecting our anger or negativity at each other, although our demands and desires take up a large bandwidth too.

While many of us restrain ourselves from verbal outbursts directed at other people, we unconsciously barrage them on an emotional/energetic level with little or no restraint. Over the span of a lifetime, we engage in thousands of negative energetic interactions, primarily on a subconscious level. We feel these exchanges, however, and our fellow humans' energy (particularly that of those we are close to) can impact us, emotionally, on different chakra levels, and over time work deep into the physical levels of our own bodies. In the same way, we can poison ourselves by holding on to these negative thought patterns.

Training in energy awareness and manipulation allows us to see this held or trapped energy and repair it, be it stagnant energy connections with others, or the bruising and injury of energetic events of their past. When we work with an energy therapist, we ask them to look into the places our system has been compromised by these energetic injuries, release the charge at the points of impact, and refill those parts of ourselves with our own highest energy.

A home or building, on the other hand, does not have the capacity to become self aware or to heal itself. And within our own home we usually feel the freedom to express our anger, fear, sadness, or grief as deeply as we actually feel it. What I find in the homes I work in is that people's long term energetic transmission sticks in the walls, in the wood, in the furniture, and in the energy body of the house itself. This deeply rooted vibrational energy remains, and affects the people who live there afterward.

While everyone is sensitive to some degree, the intensity and duration of the negative emotion expressed in a home, or even in a particular room, can seriously impair some people's ability to conduct their own energy at their optimal personal frequency. When the intensity of the vibration is extreme, this impairment may lead to illness or disturbed thought forms. In homes where people have faced great loss, long term illness such as cancer or AIDS, intense pain or anguish leading to their death, or other powerful negative experience, the stains that they leave behind can be quite palpable for those trying to live there afterward.

Our human capacity to fully let go of our lives and move on to the spirit plane is also brought into question in my work. In some of the homes to which I've been called it was impossible for the inhabitants that died to move beyond this sphere and on to a higher level. Unaware that they are dead, they remain in their home, expecting things to be the way they were during their life, holding on to the actions that held meaning for them, or desiring to resolve issues with people who are no longer available or even alive. These spirits continue with their daily (or nightly) rounds, and seem to become upset by changes that occur in their living space. Some make their presence known to the living, who to them, are invaders.

Not All About Ghosts

A lot of people want to ascribe the energetic problems of houses to "ghosts," and since the release of *Ghostbusters,* there has been tremendous interest in "ghost hunting" as well. Since I first sat down to write this book, there have been no less than a half dozen TV shows committed to Ghost Hunting, but hunting is a far cry from *healing.*

There is a cultural foundation for belief in ghosts, and I certainly find that they exist, but often when I'm working in a house, the situation is not something I can particularly relate to what I would define as such: *a presence that manifests in a location as part of its own intention to stay there, or due to its inability to transcend this plane.*

What I do find, almost invariably, is that the intense emotions or energy states that the former inhabitants emanated while they were living there, *left stains.* These stains weren't covered by paint, or wallpaper, or removed by remodeling, or any other attempts to alter the feel on the physical plane.

The *medicalization* of death, a primary spiritual process that everyone (who was lucky enough) used to conduct at home, has made death an abstraction. Death takes place in a hospital bed, the coldest, most calculated, unpleasantly sterile environment, based on our insurance company's highest or lowest standards, and for that reason, we fear it. Certainly our upbringing and cultural systems help instill a fear of death, and as the hour approaches, the great questions of our existence shake our foundations, and can make it a most difficult departure.

The difficulty that people suffer in negotiating their death, with pain-killing drugs or without, leave imprints of their deepest fears, sufferings, and longings, that remain long after they're gone. What I see at work, whether or not there is some manifest energy one would refer to as a ghost, is that the fear, pain, and anger patterns of those who died have made an imprint that affects the people who live in a house afterward.

The imprints of emotional energy are not strictly related to death, either. A number of events carry emotional impact that can create energetic templates for the home. Divorce, abuse, violence, even long-term existential malaise can contribute a feeling to a house that is palpable, and often create patterns that wind up being repeated by those who move in and find it more comfortable to act in concert with the energy than to oppose it.

Emotion Sets the Energy

How often do you allow yourself to truly express your emotions? When you see someone you love, do you hug or kiss them? In public? (What if you're not in a socially accepted relationship?) If you engage with someone you despise, do you maintain a polite front until you return to your office, car, or home, or hang up the phone? When you have a bitter disappointment, do you hold back tears until you are alone?

In my study of Chinese Medicine, I have seen firsthand the evidence of the impact unexpressed emotions have on our health. And in restricting my own emotions I have injured myself as well. We may do a good job of hiding our emotions, even from ourselves, but the neurochemical and physiological action of *having them* releases energy. Even left unprocessed, as they settle into the body, their energy continues to emanate.

Within our homes, or more often, within the privacy of our bedrooms (the only place that we can safely vent our tears, fears, anger and frustration), vortexes of stagnant energy develop. In the worst cases I have seen, where men died of AIDS, alone, having been rejected by their families, their lovers, and *themselves*, as their bodies decayed before their eyes, the stains of their emotional suffering penetrated the walls and choked off the room until it was unlivable.

On the other hand, we occasionally meet people so in love with life and invested in living it joyfully that their homes become sanctuaries. The invitation to join them for a gathering makes one's heart lift in expectation. The natural comfort and ease of being that their homes exude is a product of positive emotion, and the intention to have it expressed.

Why Nature Feels So Good

One thing I've noticed and that I find most people agree with is that you don't often find these toxic energies when you're in nature. When standing by a mighty oak, or a giant redwood, you feel the expanse, depth, protective spirit and life force energy of the tree. On the beach by the roaring ocean, we feel the pull, the cleansing churning, the wind of life force, and on top of a mountain we feel the width of the base, grounding us, even as we ascend to the point of the top. That is why man has agelessly found solace and wonder in the vastness and greatness of nature, because it is a self-healing, self-cleansing, and self-regenerating environment.

Our homes, by contrast, are not. While being extracted from the resources that nature has provided, rarely do they hold a connection to the natural elements. Therefore we feel separated from nature rather than protected by and from it. When our homes have stopped having any connection to the elements, and become repositories for the stagnant energy of those who have lived and died in them before us, the houses themselves become ill. They maintain this illness as a field, which we, by dint of our proximity, become weakened by until we are sick as well.

People's Psychic Experience

Whenever I've talked to people about my psychic work (and often it's been reluctantly, because it's bizarre even to me), the response has almost always been either an incredible opening of interest, or desire to share experience. What I've found is that people, from all walks of life and ways of thinking and being, have a story; a story of inexplicable experience, a story of a haunted house, a story of a precognitive dream, a story of the unknown.

Flying to Chicago while writing this, the woman seated next to me, Nancy, asked me what I do for a living, and I told her I was writing this book. She told me that her mother owned a house in Fresno, which had a presence they all were aware of. Whenever it entered a room, the room would turn cold. Her mother divided the house and rented rooms to college students, one of whom had a room that was frequented by this spirit. The young man engaged it in conversation, and the spirit told him its name, and that it built the house in 1898. Nancy's mother went to the hall of records to look up the information and sure enough, it was true.

Once I met a man who told me that he had gone with his family on a long drive, out to visit a relative or something, in about 1971. At this time, his older brother was in the army, in Viet Nam. As they drove down the road, perhaps 80 miles from their home, they saw a hitchhiker, and as they passed him, they all thought it was his brother, in military uniform. His father, being a rational person, didn't stop, and the vision sort of disappeared in the distance. But when they returned home the following day, the military liaison came to their house and knocked on their door, to present them the flag, and tell them that his brother had been killed.

Hearing the stories of other people, and responding to my clients constant fear that they're not OK (simply because they're aware that something is going on in their living space!), has brought it to my attention that I should publicly share my work. Letting people know exactly what I have experienced, to explain how much we are affected by our surroundings, can only benefit those who force themselves into the cultural safety of denial or unconsciousness, particularly while events around them are screaming to be paid attention to.

My Introduction to Psychic House Cleaning

At 28, in the barrel of my Saturn return, when it became apparent that the life I had been living was not working for me, I began my training at the *Academy of Intuition Medicine*®. It was my intention to gain clarity around metaphysical experiences I'd had, and to differentiate my imaginings from what might really be true sensitivity. It was at *the Academy* that I learned the fundamentals of meditation, grounding, clearing, perceiving the body as a layered energy system, energetic connections, visualization practices, focusing energy, developing a toolkit for self-examination and healing, and using it to work on myself and others. My class had a very tight bond, and met weekly off campus, to exchange readings, and help each other navigate the healing process.

It was during these readings that many of us met up with a ghost-like entity, which followed our friend Sue, when she wasn't in class. (The classroom, it turns out, was a well-protected space.) Sue felt that this ghost being had connected to her when she moved into her house, which she had felt oddly attracted to while house hunting in Marin. This spirit always appeared as a young girl, very friendly, and happy to be connected to Sue. One night at class, Sue asked if anyone would be interested in coming to her house to see if we could track the ghost and its connection there. I leapt at the offer.

While class was about figuring *myself* out, the metaphysical had been a deep interest since childhood. Magic, mystics, monsters, UFO's; I watched every episode of Leonard Nimoy's *In Search Of….* Parapsychology was one of my original ideas for a college major, but Duke University had closed their program in 1980, when I went to college. This would be my first opportunity to explore the potential existence of energy presences overlapping the physical world. Several other people volunteered to come out that Thursday night, but when the time arrived, it was simply Sue and I.

Sue showed me the house, which had been beautifully restored, and had an incredible history. It was the first house built on Mt. Tamalpais, for the daughter of a wealthy family, as a wedding gift. She lived there for most of the century, until she died in the early seventies. By then it had become somewhat run down, and was inhabited by some rather unsavory characters, who committed a number of crimes there.

Sue brought out a photo album with some pictures that had clarified the nature of the spirit's presence. She said that at Christmas she had set her living room up in a particular fashion and it just felt wrong. She liked it. It seemed correct, aesthetically, but it *felt* wrong. So she moved her all furniture and the Christmas tree around until it felt right. It wasn't the way she liked it or wanted it, but it *felt* correct. She showed me the pictures from that Christmas.

The original owner's younger sister was still living up the street, and stopped by to visit and tell Sue some of the history of the house. "Oh my, you've set the house up the very same way my sister did," she told Sue, and showed her pictures of the house from the 40s and 50s, set up at Christmastime exactly the way that Sue had rearranged things. This gave Sue an inkling of the spirit's intention; that the house would conform to its desired, static patterning.

I had no idea how to approach a house as an energy field, but in walking though it I was able to sense the some unpleasant feeling imbedded in the different rooms. Sue and I spent the evening attempting to use these feelings to see back into the history and clear the residual gunk from the events of the past. We also focused on releasing the injury that the spirit had suffered when the house was violated, by inhabitants who were not doing right, according to its intention.

Essentially, the spirit's perspective was that people had moved into its home (to which it was deeply connected, having lived there some fifty years) and begun behaving badly. The spirit wanted to protect its space, and have assurance that these things would not go on. Perhaps its presence in the house disturbed the owners who had bought it, and created a worse situation, it's hard to say. The agreement that it had made with Sue, though, for her being able to obtain the house and settle her family there, was that it would be a shared familial space. This wasn't terrifying, as these things go, but it was not an agreement Sue particularly wanted to hold on to.

I was trying to figure out how to conduct a level of energy strong enough to disconnect a spirit that had lodged for fifty-plus years in a place, and what I might tap into. Sue had traveled quite a bit, and had an amazing Indonesian Garuda mask on the wall, which struck me with its incongruity. I fell upon the idea of connecting to the mask, to the power of the Garuda, as a protector spirit, and to expanding the feeling of that Garuda throughout the house. I used it to route out all the connections that history or that the spirit had with the house, to dissolve the feelings of the history of violence, sadness, fear and anger that had come from the unpleasant people who had lived there, and to giving the woman's spirit room to depart. That Garuda amplified intention seemed to do an incredible amount of work!

One of the other interesting foci of the house was that it had been, as much of Marin was, the province of the Ohlone Indians (who had all but disappeared from the region). The backyard had an incredible view of San Francisco, and I spent some time there with its giant oak trees, trying to connect to their grounding and use it to strengthen the house's. It seemed important also to dissolve any tension between the natives' spiritual connection to the land, and the fact of the modern world that this was now a developed city. When we concluded for the evening, the house felt much better, more open, easy, and secure. Sue felt better as well, and better about being in the house.

The spirit of the little girl disappeared too, and never followed her to class again.

Knowing Your Own Home

It's unlikely that your home has that much going on, but the question is, does your home feel like a place where you can live your life fully? Can you freely laugh, cry, love, play, concentrate, work, relax, wine, dine, share, be happy, feel the warmth of the hearth and the security of four walls in the rain, defended from the outside world, connected to the things and people that you want to be connected to? Do you *want* to return to your home at the days end, after work, after travel? Is it a place that you desire to be?

Or do you feel like your house isn't really yours? As if someone else lives there, and you're just renting space? Does your house feel unpleasant? Like you have to battle for space to live, breathe, work, focus, sleep, or dream? Has your behavior (or your partner's) changed since you moved into your home? Are things that never would have been acceptable before you lived there now glossed over? Have you taken on depression, sadness or other emotional patterns that feel completely unlike you since moving into your home? A physical illness or disability? These are the kind of questions that I look at in examining how much a person inhabits their own home.

Knowing your home is a bit of a difficult objective because it requires knowing yourself to such a degree. Many of my clients dismissed the odd feelings they were beset with upon moving into their homes, for months, years, and even decades. They ignored the subtle changes that came upon them, the differences in behavior, in physical and emotional well-being, and ultimately (and to me most obviously), in the desuetude of the greater part of their homes.

My clients have abandoned master bedrooms in which they did not feel comfortable, capable of living, loving, focusing, being secure, or able to get their work done; rooms that (where I live) are worth $250,000 apiece (or were before the crash). The exchange of energy with their house is one of loss, loss that they commit to on a daily basis. But without having monitored what their energy level was like or how their physical environment should feel, it's very difficult for them to assess this as having anything to do with their home. At best, it's an irrational assumption.

Trusting Your Intuition

A fair number of my clients, some who are referred, but particularly those who find me on their own, ask me, "Would you please come to my house and tell me if there's a problem?" What they're really asking me to do, *and are truly afraid of*, is not to determine whether or not there's a ghost, but to *validate their own intuition*. My clients often suffer from tremendous cases of cognitive dissonance, as their perception battles for ground against their concept of "sanity." Invariably, when I engage in a discussion about the particular goings on, I assure them that there is some work to be done in their home, for the simple fact that they're calling me. No one gets to the point of calling me unless they have a problem.

My intuitive training was entirely focused on learning to trust one's own information. We learned to separate the channels, auditory and visual, sensory and knowing (the basic schema of energy language) and filter them into a clear understanding. My teacher's constant reminder was that "Each of you is psychic." All of us have innate perceptual capacity, but clarifying, honing, and ***listening*** to it is the key that determines our ability to use it.

If someone tells me that their unease at home relates to a sense of sadness or causes constriction in their heart, I trust their intuitive information. Although I'm well-trained and understand the language of my own intuition, I don't live in their home. My clients engage with their home's energy on a constant basis, and are much more aware of the effects than I am. They may lack a clear language to describe it, or understand it, and they may refuse to believe it, but they have their *experience.* While I can clearly tease out the relevant issues from their descriptions, I find that my clients are always the most accurate assessors of the fact that their houses are not their own.

It can be quite disturbing to have the types of experiences that my clients have had in their houses, and even more so to be forced to accept:

A: that these things really do go on, and

B: that *they* have the capacity to experience and recognize energy.

It may be even weirder to accept that some guy like me can actually correct their situation, but it's always a great relief for them, mentally and physically, when I've completed my work.

However, as they recognize the new energetic pattern that they're left with, the complete erasure of whatever had been disturbing them, and the greatly increased opportunity for them to feel their own energy, a very interesting revisioning process goes on. I often sense that their prior fear of insanity has been replaced by a somewhat nervous tickle, based on the fact that that their own intuitive understanding has been verified, and they have to engage with it as reality.

Men and Women

When I began training at *the Academy*, there were three men and fifteen women in my class. I referred to the three of us men as "the 16 percent." Throughout my years of training there, that number slowly crept up, until a decade had passed, and my teacher exclaimed that half the enrollment in her class was men!

I find men are much less likely to be drawn to this work because we are culturally trained to ignore our feelings, and intuition is about understanding your feelings, including those we don't have language for in English. As men we have a vast array of substitutions for and diversions from feeling, and we fall back into them as often as possible, so as not to be confronted by the puzzling behavior of our mates, or their demands that we reveal our vulnerability, or shame, or sadness. In our playground battles we're taught that expressing these emotions will disempower us, rather than the opposite.

While it's difficult for men to break away from the rational and anti-emotional training that we are given in this life, it can be a lifesaver. Witness the 650,000 deaths we suffer from heart disease each year. As a student of Chinese medicine, one sees the relationship between heart disease and emotional withdrawal as hand in hand, but more than that, I believe men suffer from a loss of recognition of the energy involved in their own personal and social relationships, an awareness of which could only enhance the quality thereof.

From an energy physiology standpoint, however, men are wired differently than women.

Perhaps it's our evolutionary job, as men, to be separated from feeling, as our yin and yang polarity calls for different functionality. The hunter can not afford to be empathetic with the prey, while the mother can not afford to lose connection with the child.

As men in a society, however, perhaps we've taken these structures to extremes.

The few men that were in my class were inquisitive, but the women came to class out of necessity. Many of them, in their early lives, had been trained, implicitly or explicitly, positively or negatively, to be sensitive to everything, and found it impossible to discriminate between their own feelings and the feelings of others. When in close emotional proximity to someone, they felt the feelings of that person. In friendship or relationship it became their job to tell their friend or partner or spouse what *that person* was feeling, because the partner or friend was often unaware of their own emotional material.

This constant feedback loop became intensely draining, disturbing, and often illness producing for the women who did not know how to protect their own energy field. This condition exists for many women, who unfortunately haven't had access to intuitive energy training and weren't taught that taking on the emotions of others can be habit forming and dis-ease producing.

When it comes to energetic debris in a house, women (who are wired to be more receptive to the energies surrounding them) are often overwhelmed. They're certainly more likely than men to be stricken by the negative emotional charge of whatever exists there, and left drained, emotionally shifted, unhappy, or unable to function in their normal capacity. Often they become ill from co-existing with an energy resonance that no longer belongs in their home. This sensitivity confuses and frequently annoys their rational and defended mates, however.

More than once a client requested complete discretion on my part, so that her husband would never know about my work, because for them to accept

A: the intuitions of their wife

B: their own unspoken inklings of an energetic anomaly

C: the completely bizarre concept that someone like me could have a functional capacity to alter the energy in their home was just too damaging to their rational world view and sense of control.

Invariably, after the fact, when they perceived a distinct difference in their homes, these men made comments to their wives about what unknown change she had effected to make it feel calmer, happier, prettier, fresher smelling or more spacious. It always entertained me to hear this when I checked in with my clients.

Developing Perspective

My Training in Energy Work

I ASSUME THAT MOST PEOPLE reading this book will be familiar to some extent with the concept of Energy Medicine, but the work has many flavors, so I should probably discuss a few points to help clarify how you might sense energy in your own body, and how this applies to your home or other locations.

Energy Medicine encompasses all the subtle energy healing modalities, such as acupuncture and homeopathy, but the field I was trained in, Intuition Medicine®, deals with the non-material. Intuition Medicine® is based on the premise that all matter, including human bodies, has an energetic component, which is directed by consciousness. While this concept has informed Chinese and Vedic medicine for millennia, modern physics and neuroscience is now verifying this in scientifically accepted ways.

Energy activates the atom, which magnetically aligns in the molecule, forming the base component of cellular matter, which is meticulously organized into interdependent physical systems. What we call the "energy body" is simply the organizational structure of the bio-electric fields generated by those systems. Intuition Medicine® focuses on our innate ability to intuit information from the body's energy fields and to consciously direct energy through them, thus shifting their energetic resonance, and consequently improving the physical functioning of bodily structures. Intuition Medicine practitioners learn many diagnostic and intervention tools to help heal these energy systems.

My training at *the Academy* covered the dynamics of each system, how it affected my life decisions (and vice versa), how I had applied it, injured it or left it unused. The *onion-skin theory* of energy resonance, which often calls for observing and healing injuries again and again, at depths far below the outer layer, became a byword for me, and the specific mapping of internal energy mechanisms a much needed user's manual for my body/mind/spirit.

Reconnecting myself to my body was an early affirmation of the importance of this work. Before I began my training, I was very fond of leaving my body, as means to avoid emotional or physical discomfort. Although my bones had always seemed unbreakable, the proof of my OOBEs (Out of Body Experiences) came through a wake of injuries in my teens and twenties; wrecked bikes, motorcycles, three-wheelers, cars and boats, falling off buildings, so many that I had forgotten how many injuries I had. To my surprise, my body remembered every single one, and as I worked down through the most basic levels of physical memory I was forced to recall, bodily, what I had needed to forget. It was a painful few months in class, which prepared me for working on my emotional body.(But that's another book.)

What I did ascertain from it, however, was a clear sense of the multilayered interaction of energy between ourselves and others, (and objects, which become charged with the energy we invest in them). Whether we intend to or not, we transmit energy; generally unconsciously, true, although quite powerfully when we intend to. We receive this energy and recognize it as information to be processed, or store it in our own bodies, where it can degrade our energy resonance and function, depending on the sender and their intention.

We recognize these energies in different ways, depending on the type of intuitive awareness that's most developed for each of us. Seeing, hearing, feeling, and knowing things outside our physical senses are all basic forms of intuition, developed to some degree in everyone. Because we as westerners spend so much time ignoring, doubting and negating our non-rational perceptions, we often ignore this important sense information; information that clarifies why we feel the way we feel.

Grounding Aura Chakras

These are basic building blocks of one's energy body. Our grounding is the primary level at which we connect to the earth's energy. The Earth emits magnetic waves at some 7.8 cycles per second, creating a vibrational field, the Shumann Resonance. As material byproducts of the earth, tuning ourselves (and our cells) to its frequency seems to cause great improvement in overall health. The term grounded is not solely about electricity, but in all ways indicates being of solid, secure presence.

The Aura is the body's immediate field of bio-electric energy. Its strength or weakness is an early indicator of the health of or injury to the corresponding layers in the physical and energy bodies.

Chakras are the "wheels of light" that focus the energy of the emotional centers. The Root, Navel, Solar Plexus, Heart, Throat, Third Eye and Crown (as well as hands, feet, and others, depending on specific mapping systems) conduct the physical body, emotional, personal power, compassion, communication, vision, and spirit energies. The chakras open and close in response to our capacities and life situations, and may develop connections to other people or energies via conscious or unconscious intention.

Moving Toward Space Clearing

When I began my tenure as a teaching assistant, I was stunned to see how much more complicated the whole picture was. Not only was my teacher leading the evening's meditation exercises, she was observing everyone's reaction to viewing their own emotional material, the impact that had on their body, and their effect on the room. Since much of the meditation work revolved around clearing stuck negative energy from one's systems, if nobody was cleaning, the room would fill with everyone's energetic debris, making it more difficult for anyone to maintain clarity.

It became my job to increase the grounding of the room to absorb whatever energy was being shed, gently push people who were falling out of their bodies back into consciousness, and keep everyone separate and protected from each other. All things that I had done when working directly with classmates, but for ten or twenty people at once, an energy workout unlike any I had previously considered.

I excelled in my TA position, and my teacher was quite happy with my work, so I continued for a few years. By 1996 I had sat through every class at least twice, developing a rather advanced skill set, which came in very handy when working on houses. I never felt quite as intuitively gifted as my female peers in accessing the stories or specific information that people's energy fields presented (and I feel this may be due to the different intuitive wiring of men and women), but my ability to shift energy was always highly respected.

While several of my female peers went on from *the Academy* to their own practice as intuitive consultants, as a guy, it didn't seem like something I could feature. For the most part, my friends were still as invested in self-avoidance as I had been, and I wasn't so confident that I was prepared to challenge them on this. Working on houses gave me an amazing outlet for my skills, however, and going into a house full of death was something my extremely sensitive female friends had little desire to do.

Developing Tools - Dreams

A large part of my psychic practice began with a dream. I had been traveling in Italy the day Salvador Dali died, and hopped on the next train to Barcelona to go to his museum. I decided I would get up before dawn and go to Antonio Gaudi's spectacular cathedral, the Sagrada Familia, to watch the sun rise, and take the early train to Figueres, where Dali had been entombed. I asked for a 4:30 wake up call, but awoke from this dream at 4 A.M.

I was going to Alaska, to find a long lost friend, who in real life was one of my greatest teachers. When I finally made it to his small frontier mining town, there was an amazing event taking place. Two very different sets of explorers were there, looking for two very different things.

There was a white-bearded old man, a spiritualist, with his long-haired young apprentice, seeking an ancient ritual object that they believed would bring understanding of the spiritual nature of life back into this realm. Opposite them was a group of technologists, scientists seeking a new radioactive element, that they believed would bring radical transformation to science. A completely new technology would be built upon it.

The next morning, I went down to the old abandoned mine, where both groups were seeking their lodestones, and I hiked down the mineshaft to a point where another tunnel intersected it. I stood there at this lightless crossing and saw, from my left, the old man and his apprentice approaching me, holding a glowing gold, horseshoe like object. It was an ancient torc, the ornate Celtic neck-ring symbolizing nobility, offered by Cernunnos, god of animals. It was obvious that this object carried incredible spiritual power, and awareness for our civilization.

At the same time, from my right, the technologists approached, with their leader holding an apparently radioactive stone, about the size of a softball, shining green in the darkness. Each lit by their object, the two groups came together at the intersection of the tunnels, and studied at each other. The technologist reached out his glowing stone, and the spiritualist reached out the prongs of his torc, and they touched them together, right in front of me.

The objects locked together, fusing in an atomic explosion that bore through us with blinding light before it dissolved everything. In infinite slow motion, I was witness to the birthing of a new sun. I could feel each of my atoms being ripped apart by this expanding fireball of unbelievable heat, which blew me across the galaxy, in all directions, until the points of my consciousness were flung millions of miles apart in space.

I did not wake up. I floated, for what seemed tens of thousands of years, until I became so cold from floating in the very depths of space that all of my atomic material contracted back into *me*, and I found myself in my body, laying naked in the snow. Under a pitch black sky showered with stars, I lied there, wondering, *"Did I survive that just so I could freeze to death?"* Then a door opened, a hundred yards away. I could see firelight inside, so I got up, and began walking toward it. As my eyes adjusted to the starlight, I could see that I was back in the town, and that the open door led into a bar. My friend was waiting there. He looked at me, with his sly, knowing smile, and asked, "Can I get you a drink?" Then I woke up.

So how do I use this dream as a tool?

The feeling of standing within an atomic explosion is one that I don't imagine most people have experienced, but by dint of being there, in my dream, I feel I can recreate, and transmit on some level. As my meditation practice evolved to suit my work, I realized that I needed to develop power tools such as this, the kind I wouldn't think of using on a person. I couldn't have sought them specifically, they each came from the realization that I could translate the feeling of certain experiences into vibration.

Energy Signatures

In much the same way, I've taught myself to keep track of the energetic resonances of natural spaces. I've made it part of my career to go to power spots and meditate, log the sense/feeling of their particular vibrational field, store it in my memory, and be able to generate it when I need it. These filed field energies allow me to bring much greater power to clearing and grounding spaces.

Some resonances that I've found particularly useful are Mount Shasta, Mount Denali, Yosemite and its waterfalls, Jumbo Rock in Joshua Tree, Avebury and Glastonbury (although not so much Stonehenge), or the Humboldt Redwoods, In all of these places Nature's commanding presence is overwhelming. One is not merely smitten by their grandeur, one feels a change in state as they enter their vibrational field. The grounding is so strong in these places that it easily resets yours.

Of course, one needn't climb Everest to feel a connection to nature, or its healing energy. Sitting in the park for long enough to be aware of its pull may be just the reminder you need to be in your body. But when we return to our houses, after a day in the world, we often feel weakened, discharged, ungrounded, and our homes rarely supply any reconnection with the planet. Particularly now, with all the EMF generation, television, radio waves, and our own wireless computer and cell phone signals, the amount of radiation that is passing through our bio-electric field without our notice can be quite disturbing.

The amount of turmoil in our day-to-day lives too, with the complications of work, family, love, and money, rarely lets us feel like we're at home in a safe, protected, restorative place, which is what our home should be. If our home is out of whack to begin with, it can be impossible to really feel comfortable there. Conducting the vibrational feel of a strong earth energy generator lets me bring a house back into grounded alignment, and is a major part of my work.

Vibratory Attraction

Fairly early in my training I noticed that I had a different sensitivity to energy than my female classmates. (Perhaps it could be better described as *in*sensitivity.) Part of learning the language of energy is identifying the different types of healing energies, the personal and universal, and using them to heal oneself.

One of the primary energies that we learned about was Kundalini. I was fairly proficient at running Kundalini, I could feel it raising my temperature and activating my chakras, but the women in class were having radical experiences. They would suffer emotional upheavals, be unable to sleep for days, have out of body experiences, the kind of things that made me feel jealous and wonder if I was really getting it.

As it turned out, I was, but my system had been "cored out" to a higher gauge. Reflecting on my youth, it was obvious why, I had always sought out experiences of high vibrational intensity. Loud music, certainly, but I also had a penchant for climbing high tension towers, and getting as close as I could to the wires. It was still easy to recall the feeling of all my hair standing on end as the current electrified my body. Another favorite was to climb inside a railroad trestle bridge at night, using the trapdoor that dropped under the tracks, and hiding there until the freights rumbled over at 80 miles an hour, shaking you to your marrow. Over time, I suppose that my sensitivity increased, as my searches led to more esoteric vibrations.

Office Work

After finishing my training in Chi Nei Tsang (specific form of Chinese medical massage in which you massage your client's abdominal organs, which can release a lifetime of held emotional energy), I began developing my bodywork practice. I sublet my intuitive counselor friend's office and started inviting clients.

Not wanting to leave a trail of emotional/energetic debris in my friend's office, I began clearing her office when I was done working, so it was clear for her to return to. I realized that I needed to maintain an extra heavy-duty grounding system to absorb the energy that was being released there, as well as keep my clients clear from hers.

Being an astute intuitive, she began to comment on the clarity of her office when I was done, and I worked with her on developing this energy protocol. Other friends who did intuitive work had me look at their offices and realign the grounding for them.

Some were starting their practices in offices they rented, and finding that within people's therapy or bodywork offices, a sense of fullness, or density of energy existed. It was obvious that people came to these offices to dump, leaving their emotional, psychological and physical negativity in offices that were intended for that task. It was apparent to us, however, that the people running those offices had no understanding of the energy dynamic that they were creating.

The day after day therapy, bodywork, or healing sessions drained the clients' negative energy, and I'm sure relieved them greatly. But it filled these offices with more and more negative energy, until the space itself was noxious. This is unhealthy for the practitioner, and becomes uninviting for the clients. Without grounding off the energy that their clients were releasing, the practitioners in these office spaces were creating toxic dumping grounds of the first degree. Fortunately for my friends, I was developing the means to correct this.

In the Kitchen

When I began thinking about doing housework professionally, I took out an ad in a new-agey paper, but the phone did not jump off the hook. The sporadic client flow that ad brought in barely paid for the printing. In 1996 I decided that to take my work to a professional level, I should start connecting with realtors. I found a real estate listings magazine, and while meditating, looked through it to determine which houses had not been selling. Amazingly, the magazine popped open to a picture of Sister Sue's house, so I gave her a call, as it had been a few years. She told me that yes, she was selling her house, and it had been on the market for months with no offers. This was before every house in the Bay Area was selling for a fortune, we had finally recovered from the 1989 earthquake, but Sue's house *was* listed for a million dollars. I told her what I was up to and she asked me if I might be able to help.

When I got to the house, I was expecting to have to review the imprint of the former owner, the impact of the murder that had taken place there, the negative energy from the wild scene of the '70s, but there was none of that. I had cleaned all that years before. What I did find, quite oddly, was that energy from the neighbor's house was coming into Sue's and disrupting the energy.

This was almost inconceivable to me, that a force from outside could be so invasive, but it was early in my career. I asked Sue if there had been any kind of negative situation with the neighbor. As it turned out, shortly after Sue moved in, this neighbor (Mrs. X) began a multi-year construction project, endlessly remodeling and expanding, which had upset the entire neighborhood. The street was constantly blocked, construction crews were in and out, trucks, equipment, noise, until the entire block was pissed off.

Sue recalled that when she had first purchased her home, Mrs. X seemed to be quite angry with her. It turned out that Mrs. X had been very close to the woman who had sold the house to Sue. This friendship and the time spent in what would become Sue's house had given Mrs. X to a great desire to own it, whether for its somewhat better view, greater size, history, or value, I'm not sure, but Mrs. X had felt slighted and angry that Sue was able to purchase it away from her, and had to tear her own house apart to try to even up the score.

Because she had spent so much time in the house over the years before Sue owned it, it appeared to me that Mrs. X had her own energy entrance. It was like a corridor, from one back kitchen door to the other, but more penetrating, like a tunnel. Through the fence, through the walls, Mrs. X had a virtual energy presence in Sue's house, based on her past time agreement with the previous owner. She knew the kitchen, the living room, the floor plan, the views, she had spent a great amount of time as a guest and also imagining herself as the owner. But now that Sue was selling, she was faced with not owning it again, and her ire over that pushed her to "spike" the house. Whether consciously or unconsciously, or both, Mrs. X was able to direct her negative energy into Sue's house, and that was making it impossible to sell.

I was getting used to the idea that dead people left their energy in a house, and that their energy made it uncomfortable for the people who succeeded them, but I hadn't considered that the impact of a living person (particularly one outside the family) could be so palpable. Mrs. X was everywhere in that house, so I collected her energy and returned it to her, next door. I reset the house so as to no longer give her ingress, built special layered protection between the houses, and when I walked through the house, I could no longer feel her. Done. When I called Sue that Saturday, she told me she had shown the house to one person that Friday, and he offered them a million for it.

That was when I realized, *I **am** a pro!*

The House As An Energy Structure

When we look at the energy body of a person, we discuss the energy structure in levels, the aura, the chakras, the grounding channel, the Chinese energy meridians, and also the physical structures, the skeletal and organ structures, as being resonances, vibrational fields, or yin condensations of energy into matter.

When I first went to Sue's house I wondered what it would look like energetically. I assumed it would have a layered structure with a central core, something like the energy body of a human. My assumption was quickly disproven, however, although there are some similarities.

A house has a certain flow of energy to it, and while architectural features (or flaws) and directional alignment have a lot to do with it, the most important things are that it is *grounded and protected.*

Grounding varies quite a bit from house to house, neighborhood to neighborhood, city to city, and client to client. It can even be split within a house. A solid rocklike grounding imbues a house with a kind of certainty, calm, and clarity. The lack thereof (which is much more frequent) makes things feel floaty, out of balance, precarious, unsafe, and actually be somewhat accident inducing.

From the outside, one notices the overall feel a house exudes, which obviously has something to do with its appearance, but also displays its *protective layers*. Some houses feel like you could just walk in, grab a beer out of the fridge, spill some on the couch, order a pay-per-view movie, fire up a cigar, and start making long distance phone calls. That's not an energetically protected house.

When I work on a house, I look for *conformity of energy*. The conformity of energy within the house is only noticeable when you walk through. Is there an even flow, without transition, from room to room, in the *feel* of the house? Do certain rooms seem disconnected, uneven, hotter, cooler, or compromised?

Obviously, a major cause for a room to feel sick is the *residual energy* from previous dwellers. I try to sense whether the house feels associated with the people who live there, or someone else, which is not hard to do. Unpleasant feelings or sensations in a particular room or rooms usually give it away.

House themselves seem to carry *contracts* for how they are to be lived in. These can hold a great deal of energy, and connection to those who've lived there before.

There are *external factors* that can create a disturbance in the way someone would choose to live in their house, or in dealing with the house itself. A house may be affected by someone else's focused energy, or a historic sense thereof.

The house itself may have an *imbedded attitude,* which may be from a combination of the issues I've already mentioned.

Last (for me to have discovered) but not least, a house has an *astral address.* This is the location of your house in your dreams, which can be extremely important, when others are dreaming about your house.

Grounding

Grounding is our energetic connection to the Earth's vibrational field. It's how we release negative energy and restore our own positive energy, keeping us healthy and vibrant. A house is built on the ground or into the ground, and without a solid grounding, or with something blocking the grounding, it won't feel very comforting. When the grounding of a house is blocked, its ability to exist in optimal vibrational clarity is compromised, and it can feel sickly, unsupported, or collapsed, like it's not breathing.

What makes a house's grounding functional?

Intention, of course, is primary. It's unlikely that you have performed any ritual to claim your house and direct it to your purposes, but if the house isn't grounded to you, your family, and your intention for life, what is its grounding set for? Another person, or family, often with a set of life circumstances that you'd prefer not to repeat, is what I find. Location can do a lot for grounding too. A house in a natural setting with room to breathe has a lot more potential for being grounded than a tract home or one crowded in by an overgrown city.

What makes a house's grounding dysfunctional?

Obviously, the energy of any dead people still residing in a house can affect its grounding, but all of the negative emotional energy that has accumulates over its history may be even more detrimental. Was the property sold out of probate? Was there family dissent? A bankruptcy? Perhaps the land was stolen, from natives, and built over? Was the house converted from a storefront, a school, a farm, a factory, a warehouse, a graveyard, a toxic waste site? Something intended for a purpose other than you and your family living there? Many times (what later becomes) a house is built with an intention unsuited to being a living space, and its grounding is unsuitable to living there as well.

Protection

While I started out looking for an aura around the houses I worked on, and to some degree could say that's what I found, what I really see in terms of the aura of a house is its protective layer. Just because we have walls around us doesn't mean we've invested them with the energy to really defend us. Gated community or not, some houses *feel* like secure, protected space, while others have the distinct feeling of being transparent, as if everyone outside can look in. Many times our houses are so close together they seem wall-less to begin with, and when we haven't defined energetic layers on our perimeter we can be unduly influenced by the actions of our neighbors, or people who don't even live near us. Good fences make good neighbors, and energetic layers make your home feel like a place you can live without intrusion.

Conformity of Energy

When a structure is built, it's constructed in a certain period of time with certain owners and their intentions for living there. When an addition is built, it's usually done by a different family or owner, in a different situation. By the time the addition is made, the owner is no longer working with the same piece of land. Time has passed, the planet has moved, and the grounding has changed, so the sections of the building can feel completely disconnected.

Built as a cabin in 1905, and added on to in the '50s, Mark's house felt "off kilter" to him. He had done a lot of work to restore it, but called me because there were a number of disturbances there and he had just cleared out his problem tenant, an alcoholic with whom he had been in some altercations. That created some negative feeling about the property, or perhaps just brought them to the surface. In either case, he wanted them resolved.

When I went to the house, I realized very quickly that feeling of the front section of the house, the original cabin, and the addition, which was just about as large, felt completely different. This was the first time I noticed the difference in the grounding between sections of a house.

Walking between the two sections of Mark's house felt like moving between two entirely different houses. It wasn't that the floors weren't level or the angles weren't true, it simply felt as if you had left the house and entered a different one.

The remnant energy of Mark's tenant (and the entities he had attracted from his alcohol bingeing) had to be cleared first, but wasn't too hard. Integrating the sections of the house was where the job really began. The two phases of a) creating a new and contiguous grounding for the whole property, with a core for the full dimensions of the house, and b) fusing the two sections of the house into one whole, with a new contract for ownership, totally changed the dynamic and feel of the place.

The Contract

The thing that I first uncovered (that I least expected to find in the energetic structure of a house), is what I call the contract. There appears to me to be a contract for living in a house. The first contract, the boilerplate for living in a house, is set up by the first people who establish residence. In situations where people have designed or built their home themselves, with a certain intention or vision for their family, the homes are very much in agreement with what they were trying to achieve. But in this society I find that situation to be quite rare.

For the most part people move into a house that was built in a tract somewhere and simply attempt to live their lives. Intention being key to everything in this work, I find that their houses sort of stumble along with their life path, setting up the contract for living there in accordance with the life events that take place. When tragedy strikes, with divorce, death, illness, or abuse, these issues become contracted to how a house expects its residents to live. When a new family moves in they find themselves drifting toward the same behaviors, incidents, or outcomes.

I've had a number of cases where my client moved in to find that the previous tenant had the same number of children, the same ideas for remodeling, the same sleazy affair with the best friend, and would up with the same divorce. Some houses seem to call their tenants to die, because the contract with the previous or original owner was to be a place in which to die. The contract between a house and its tenants is extremely important to the way their lives there will be played out, and calls for serious examination and renegotiation (preferably by a member of the psychic bar association).

I'm not certain, in cases where tenants repeat the contracted behaviors, whether they choose their house because it feels like the place to complete their karmic destiny, or whether it's just easier to align themselves to the contract than to intentionally create their lives. I do know that my old clients almost always call me to clean the houses they move to, because they don't want to find out later what they've inadvertently aligned themselves with.

Residual Energy

The residual energy of a house is directly related to the intensity of the emotional/energetic events that have occurred there. Houses hold energetic imprints. Particularly those in which there has been some form of abuse, physical or emotional, fear, suffering, serious pain, lingering disease, cancer or AIDS, or simply death itself (when not viewed or undertaken with a certain level of consciousness). These stains stick, in the walls, in the woodwork, in the energy field, and they don't go away with scrubbing, painting, or remodeling. Energy stains make it difficult for the people who move into such a home to bring their own energy in, or to develop new contracts with the house for living at their own highest potential, because the vibrational capacity of the home has been filled with the residue of those who have lived, and often died there.

When I look at the residual energy of a house, I try to examine the first owners or track the person or family that has left the most intense stains. Then I look at the people who came after them and before them, although the major stains are usually the majority of the job. What I sometimes find is that different rooms will have different charges relating to different tenants. It may be that the bedroom on the West was chosen by one family and the bedroom on the North by another. The activities or deaths that occurred in those different rooms hold different feelings, different connections, and different energies.

As the energies in different rooms indicate the nature of the events and the person(s) from whom they were released, we get different sensations from different rooms. My clients often feel more comfortable in one room than another, and choose that room over the other, leaving the first unused, despite its hefty price tag.

In my attempts to key into each of the energy signatures that I find in the residual energy, I'll track down the members of the energetically related family and dissolve whatever emotional connections they may have had to a particular event. This often disrupts the link that my client's family may have with them, constellating around the house's contract for its inhabitants to relive a particular kind of event.

Imbedded Attitudes

Some homes seem to have less of a feeling of illness or death as simply a position on life from which they cannot be swayed. If a prior tenant has held a strong enough attitude of reclusiveness, anger, judgment, disdain, fear, depression, or anxiety, it can build up in a house and leave a noticeable imprint. One may find it difficult to overcome, or find it easier to assume the attitude, even though it doesn't agree with their personality, just to feel at ease in the house.

Externals

What I was quite surprised to find, but glad I stumbled upon fairly early in my career, is that people outside your home can have a direct influence on it. You've heard of the nosy neighbor, well, sometimes their nose is stuck in your laundry room. Often the neighbor doesn't even live next door anymore. Since the house has established its own contracts, the agreements or disagreements between the tenants and other families in the neighborhood form attitudes *between the houses*. When you move in, you find that you're immediately disdainful of the family living at 2367, who had an ongoing row with the family that lived in your house. The contract between your houses give them the impression that simply by living in your house that you are a snob, or untrustworthy, or whatever sort of attitude was engaged in by the prior tenants. By contract, you are now engaged in this old dispute, without having any input whatsoever as to the relationship you want to have.

There are array of external factors, not the least of which may be family members. In inherited homes, siblings and relatives have their own intimate connection to the home's energetic history, and thereby to your life there. Any number of factors or outside sources of energy may affect your home, from (un) natural phenomena, to negotiating the sale of your home, and working with realtors or buyers. I'm sure I haven't seen the last of the oddities that can keep your home from feeling like your own and maintaining the energetic alignment you would like to have.

Astral Address

One of the energy bodies we discuss in a human being is the Astral body, the part of us that takes over during sleep and communicates with us and everyone else on the dream plane. It took me some years in my practice before I fully recognized the impact of the astral plane on a house, and its inhabitants. Think of a house as a way station, if you will, a place where the inhabitants not only live their daily lives, but sleep and live their dream lives. Recognize then that this house must have an astral address, a location from which dream bodies depart and to which they return.

Imagine there is someone you wish to know, or who wishes to know you. Perhaps you seek them in your dreams, or they seek you. Do you meet in neutral territory, or do they arrive at your house? Now think of all the people you know, and have relationships with, that you see in dreams. How many of them have an astral key to your house? Everyone who's ever lived in your house, or simply visited it, has an astral entry point of their own. People who have nothing to do with your life, who have no conscious recollection or knowledge of your living space, can enter it through their dreams.

In the worst of cases, the astral level is where those who no longer have a body return to the home that they still believe is theirs, and meet the new inhabitants in a most direct and unpleasant manner.

Owning vs Renting

One of the stickiest wickets of this business is the question of ownership and responsibility. Many of my clients rent their homes, and it becomes a major decision for them to hire me. It's not like calling the landlord to fix the roof (which can be hassle enough), it's an investment in a home they don't own. Would you call your landlord to tell him that his property felt like death, and that you want to have it cleaned, at his expense? Probably not, *but you could give him this book as a subtle hint.*

If the landlord has any knowledge of something unpleasant about their property, they're usually trying to ignore it, avoid it, sidestep it, and go on with the rational belief that it doesn't exist. An absentee landlord, of course, may have never even lived there, and has no connection to the property whatsoever. In the end, it pretty much comes down to the question of whether they would make some effort to repudiate your claim, or simply accuse you of being a whacko.

In a very few cases, my clients' landlords have split my fee with them, and one time they admitted (after the fact) that they knew the rental was haunted, but generally, the expense of living with it falls on the renter, which is truly unjust. The way I see it, the owner has the primary contract with the property. Whether it's an old family property, a house they lived in and moved up from, or strictly an investment, their contract and emotional connection to it can determine what sort of energy is invested in the property, and whether the dwelling sees itself as a home or simply a financial vehicle.

With the owner in absentia, the renter, who really has the least power in changing things, winds up with the burden of negotiating the contract. Since the renter technically is outside the loop, a third party, as it were, I've always looked at the ethics of renegotiating the owner's contract to the house. Of course, I am also talking to the house, and having to take its viewpoint in to account. I generally find that respect for and responsibility to their property bodes well for landlords, in terms of whom they'll attract and what care tenants will take. From there, it's not too far to bring the renter into the agreement with the dwelling. As the primary inhabitant, who will fill the space with their own energy, they definitely have a connection to be facilitated.

Apartments vs Houses

Not all my clients have houses, either. A moderate percentage of my work goes on in apartments. When I first got called to heal an apartment I thought, "No problem, it's half the size of a house! I'll be done in no time." What I didn't consider was that the apartment was *inside a larger building,* surrounded by other apartments, all sharing the same non-functional grounding. Of course, the fact my client's apartment was formerly a junkie haven, where someone had died from an overdose, was par for the course.

Apartments in themselves have a similar energy structure to houses, but their inclusion in a larger set of living spaces makes grounding, protection, and neighbor issues much more challenging. The negotiation of common space, boundaries, and noise, can quickly point you to the fact that your home is not "yours." High rise apartments have an annoying tendency (for lack of grounding) to feel "floaty," or swaying in the breeze, while apartments with a high turnover feel impossible to settle into.

Your contract to the apartment, which, as a renter, is via agreement with the landlord, also factors in. And while the energy imprints of former tenants may be more superficial, due to the transient nature of their inhabitation, some people live 20 or more years in an apartment, and die there too, so there's no dismissing the fact that yours may not feel like home.

Your House

Does *Your* House Feel *Off*?

PEOPLE ARE ALWAYS ASKING ME, when I visit their homes, to tell them if I feel anything weird. "No," I say, "only you." I don't go searching for work in my quotidian mode. I don't wander around or go to parties with my sensitivity heightened, lurking for energetic dissonance. It would be extremely loud. Certainly, some places smack with residue, but part of the reason I'm as good as I am at what I do is that I can ignore it.

I am somewhat hesitant to write this chapter, because I don't want to plant any ideas in your head about what might be wrong with your house or have you searching for evidence. The key to determining whether something is going on in your home is whether you *can't* ignore it. The elephant in the room things will be obvious to you, and are completely different from house to house and situation to situation. The little things I'll mention here frequently come as afterthoughts to my clients, they're the ah-haaaas that tie a minor or ignored odd feeling into the larger picture. These are the things that I look for, because they indicate a problem to *me*, primarily non-conformity of energy.

Indicators

The first thing that I notice in a house is usually Headroom. Some rooms feel as if the ceiling is a foot lower than it should be. I'll feel a weight on the top of my head in these rooms, and will ask the client if they are apt to get *headaches* there. Although they rarely notice the height problem, they often do get headaches or feel uncomfortable there, making the room one to be avoided.

Pressure Difference is another related symptom that I look for. Going through a house, some rooms will feel as if the atmospheric pressure is denser than others. Of course, one has to account for temperature and air flow, but in rooms that are affected, the sluggish sometimes taffy-like quality has no physical cause.

Everyone has seen a spooky movie where a **Cold Chill** pervades a room, but when you actually have the sensation that something cold has overtaken you, in a warm room, or have a room which inexplicably won't heat, despite a functioning furnace and an otherwise warm house, it can be an indicator that something or someone does not want you to share the space.

Far rarer but much more unpleasant are **Smells**. From the old-woman's perfume to the dead guy's cigarette, the fact that the smells of former inhabitants are somehow activated by their presence is one of the truly mysterious and unnerving things about these phenomena. Air cleaner, carpet shampoo, open windows, incense, nothing stops these smells from appearing, out of nowhere, at random times or with clocklike regularity.

Electrical and Telephone Problems, while fairly common on the one hand, are fairly uncommon on the other. When your phone and power inexplicably cut on and off, appliances turn themselves on and off, and the phone and power companies have sent technicians over that have found nothing, it's not about the wires. The houses that have had the worst incidence of this, that I've seen, were the sites of suicides. In fact, in almost all the cases of poltergeist activity (physical movement of objects) that I've worked on, there had been a suicide in the house.

Feeling Unlike Yourself, specifically anxious, possibly depressed, may also be an indicator. It's a pretty broad statement and I'd hate to hang my profession on that per se, but what I've ascertained from my clients is that when these feelings are specifically related to being in their new house, felt only when inside the house, don't resolve over time, and result in adaptive behavioral changes they may be related to something other than your true self.

My Clients

We live in a culture born out of a rationalistic mindset. I was born into it. I certainly invested myself in rationalism and scientific knowledge, to the point of denying any experiences which I might have considered spiritual. So beginning this work was difficult for me, and is still somewhat odd. I think my average client finds it very hard to embrace the reality of what they experience, sensorially, mentally, and emotionally, in dealing with the kind of situations that get me called to work.

Mind you, I'm something of a court of last resorts guy. Many of my clients have done simple clearing procedures, burned sage, prayed, told the spirits to leave, some even had other people come and try to clear their house, unsuccessfully, but almost all of them denied, again and again, that the various activities were happening. When they give up trying to put a rational face on things (and some come to a point where they feel they are actually losing their minds), they find me. Somehow, they find me. Because they need someone to assure them that what is happening is happening, and *they need me to fix it!*

A lot of clients call me and ask me if I will come to their house and tell them whether they have a problem. For me, this is a rather ludicrous question, because it's obvious to me that if they've gotten to the point of finding and then *calling* me, THEY HAVE A PROBLEM! Besides that, for me to come to their house and tell them — "Yes, you have a problem that only I can fix. Hire me." — would be completely unethical.

I know that *they are psychic* too, and on a human level, it's most important for me to validate the reality of what they're experiencing. I help my clients understand that their intuition, and more than that, their actual grounded-in-reality experience of having an energetically problematic house, is real. Once that's settled, it's my job as House Healer to resolve whatever their situation is, and make their house feel like brand new, or better.

A Story That Fits The Feeling

Sometimes clients ask me if I can tell them the names and dates and histories of the former residents, and provide a blow by blow psychic reading of the events that occurred in their house, sort of an ... *if you're so psychic, prove it.* So, in my best Sam Spade voice, I tell them, "I'm not that kind of psychic, babe."

It's not that I'm not interested. We all want a story, to try to understand just what's happening and why. Generally, I find my clients' intuition reliable, though, and I use their description of the feelings and events, or what bits of history they've been able to cobble together from previous owners and/or neighbors, to create some kind of narrative that allows me to address the situation. It helps me keep on track, and envision the energy I'm dealing with.

In many cases, my client has no information at all about the house, or its history, and it's something of a feel-around bit of guesswork. If I took the time to try to read their entire house and its history, and check that against the city records and newspapers, I'd be there all week, and that would be *really* expensive.

It's not that the particulars don't matter, but it's unlikely that we'll ever really know exactly what happened. Sometimes I intuit things that my client forgot to tell me, or had never thought about, and when I query them about it, it brings their awareness to it, and that brings the work more into focus. I definitely try to get as much information as possible because it helps us construct a story that fits the feeling, which is a basic human need.

While part of the work is about affirming my clients' sense of what is going on, and how it relates to the past, some clients would prefer not to know, and some situations are strictly about getting the job done. Of course, getting the job done, is what I'm all about.

How I Work

I'm often asked what I do when I go to a house, whether I carry feathers, or rattles, burn sage or ring bells, (play the kazoo — wear flowing robes, etcetera, etcetera), and again I have to say "I'm not that kind of psychic, babe." My method is strictly one of meditatively conducting energy. I meditate, on some jobs for up to five hours (or even overnight in special cases), expanding my awareness to perceive the energies present in a house, resolve their issues, and dissolve their remnants. It's a layered process for which I've developed a step-by-step approach.

From the outset, I try to prepare myself for entering the situation as described by my client, and potentially encountering things that they have not perceived. (In my early outings I ran into some powerful forces that I was not prepared for, and it wasn't pleasant, so preparation has become essential for me.) This means several days of increased meditation, and abstinence from alcohol or any medication that might disturb my sleep or waking state.

Arriving at a jobsite, I'll make sure I'm grounded and set my personal protection, then examine the energy of the building and its surroundings, and set up a protective field around them, so that whatever is inside stays there. It often reminds me of that *Exorcist* moment, with Max von Sydow standing outside the house, anticipating the job within *(complete with twinkly Exorcist theme music)*. Then I laugh at myself and go to meet my client, who is usually spinning some combination of trepidation, fear and hope. I'll have them guide me through the house, detailing the particular problem spots and filling in any details that we haven't covered.

Even while we're talking I may be working on grounding the house, pulling local earth energy through the floor and running it through the entirety of the house, and beyond to fill the protective field. From there I'll find a good spot to meditate, and enter into a dialogue with the house itself. This is where I gather information about the events that have set the tone for living and the house's relationships with the parties involved. Using my "psychic attorney" skills, I alter these contracts to suit the present time reality. This relieves the house of the need to hold on to old patterns, and frees up connected energies to be moved out.

From the contract I tend to look at the held energy of a house.

When we talk about the human as a bio-electric field, we move past the rationalistic medical model of the body and into a cellular communication model, an innately intelligent structural organizational model, a quantum or vibrational model, based on the fact that all of these structures are conducting energy on their own wavelengths, communicating with each other and with energy directing them from higher levels.

When we look at a house, we can see it as a collection of inert objects: wood, wallboard, glass, plastic, pipe, fixtures, *ducts!*, or we can relate to the actual molecular principle that all of these things are made up of atoms that are still in constant motion.

What I see in the energetic field of any room in a particular house is the imprint of the emotional energy that has been transmitted by the bioelectric fields of the people who lived there, and become lodged in the vibrational field of the woodwork, the wallboard, the furniture, and in the energetic field of the house itself.

I move from room to room, examining and clearing the energy patterns from each as I sit in them, but I've also developed the capacity to sit in one place and observe the entirety of the house, which helps me to see the connections. Depending on what has happened in a house, there may be more than one actor or event to deal with. In older houses, perhaps two different families had deaths occur, at different times in different rooms, and the connections between the members of each family and the rooms they lived in will carry different energy patterns and intensities. Looking at the overall field I decide where I want to start clearing. Having found that the initial incident sets the tone for everything that follows, I usually start on the easier stuff and work my up to it.

Then it becomes a process of either encountering extant spirits, negotiating their reasons for being there and crossing them over to a higher plane, and/or reading and clearing the energetic imprints that they've left behind, as well as any kind of entities that have piggybacked their way in on the current of held emotion. This goes on from room to room and situation to situation, and may call for my sitting in a particular room to engage the energy there and be certain it's cleared.

From there I look at outside influences, clearing neighbors or even the client's family members who have invested their energy in the house, and restoring the boundaries to a functional distance. I also look to the astral level, where access to the house is open to all that have passed through it, and others, who may affect the dreams of my client. With the house's new contract for living set in place, none of these situations are permissible, and resolving them sets the tone for elementally resetting and rebuilding the house.

Five Element Wash

What I believe sets my house healing work apart from others' is my focus not just on clearing out whatever has been causing problems, but on rebuilding the house from the grounding up. Much as vibrational healing for people has to do with re-visioning the body as a vibrational structure, and using all sorts of imagery and energy to enhance its capacity, resetting the vibrational structure of a house is essential to making it the *home* my clients desire. I dismantle and rebuild every house, energetically, wiping it clean and structurally bringing it to its highest energy level. This process makes the house feel incredibly clean and positive.

In fact, it's what I do when I travel, and have to stay somewhere that I don't have time or interest in really cleaning, like a hotel room. Weigh stations like that have tremendous energy built up, that can send my dreams all over the map. If I weren't so particular about taking care of the details of my work I could clean a house in a third of the time just by doing a five element wash. Since it really isn't engaging any of the specific energies that may be residing in your house, it's probably safe to do on your own, although it takes a significant amount of concentration.

The process started out of an essential pagan process of calling the four directions. I would invite in the forces of Fire, Water, Air, and Earth, visualizing each in its most powerful nature form, to burn, wash, blow out and ground the entirety of the house. This seemed to work fairly well, but my study of Chinese science really made it take hold.

Taoist science sees the world in terms of yin and yang, and *five* elements, Wood, Fire, Earth, Metal and Water, which are clearly related to each other in an ordinal (birth) pattern, as well as others. Wood burns, making Fire, whose ashes make Earth, in which is found Metal, which condenses Water, which feeds Wood. As I've said before, I like to travel to natural places to get a sense of their particular grounding, but I also go to feel of nature in its raw form, which is what I try to project throughout a house in order to do this level of clearing. I've meditated in the face of huge waterfalls, on the burls of giant redwoods, on top of massive boulders, and with my crystal collection (which ain't half bad). I've also survived my house burning down, and (as I described in my dream) been atomized in a fusion reaction. These experiences have all become part of my *toolkit*.

If you want to try this on your own home, keep in mind that the intensity of the image you can project will determine the level of effect you have. To begin a five element process, start with Fire. Imagine a flame at your center and expanding it through your entire home. I use the image of the sun, explosions, or forest fire engulfing everything and burning out every trace of memory, until I can feel nothing left but a pile of ash.

From that ash, I bring in the Earth energy, in the shape of a mountain, growing and expanding throughout the entire space of the structure (or where the structure would be if I hadn't burnt it down). When the space is filled with grounded earth, I begin to sift it for Metal, and pull from it columns of gold, silver, and copper. I use these to build a framework of energy on which I grow crystals, quartz, amethyst, citrine, tourmaline, diamonds, emeralds, sapphires, conducting every color of crystal energy that I can think of, or feels appropriate for a particular room.

Condensing Water of the surfaces of the metals and gems, I let it build from a trickle to a stream, to a river, to a waterfall the size of Vernal, or Tuolumne, or Rancheria, huge falls in Yosemite whose force would atomize your entire house. I run this water through the space until I feel the ionic freshness, after which I follow the stream down into the forest, where I begin to grow Wood.

Having spent hours and hours in tree meditation, I can easily install the feel of mighty oaks, majestic redwoods, and sturdy pines. From there I work my way into the grasses and flowers, filling the space with tulips, roses, gardenia, magnolias, foxglove and dahlias, every shape and color of *living plant energy* I can think of. By the end of this whole process, which can take anywhere from five minutes to an hour, the space I'm working on has been reformatted so many times that it feels completely fresh and new, and I can rebuild it from scratch, layering it with energetic building materials.

My Guarantee – *Things Change*

It's always been impossible to quantify or scientifically *verify* what I do, so I've always offered my clients a full guarantee, on the front end. Since the work was so *inconceivable* to begin with, I always let my clients pay me half up front, and then send me the rest after *they themselves were certain that something had changed.* On occasion, there was some touch up that I needed to address, and did, but invariably, things changed, which worked well for both of us.

Ethics

When I began doing this work, I went at it pretty cowboy, using the skills I had to pretty much blow things out. In dealing with some houses that were inhabited by clearly defined spirits, I realized this was somewhat disrespectful, and began to engage them and attempt to resolve their reason for remaining, which made helping them depart a cinch. Over time, I also came across situations that challenged me to make ethical decisions in a situation where there were no definitions. I've always considered myself a pretty ethical guy, and don't want bad karma that could easily be avoided, so I wound up creating rules on the fly.

Since my work covers the gamut of human relationships, the need occasionally arises for me to weigh my client's wish for resolution against the need to maintain the integrity of other parties' connections and contracts. For instance, I'm occasionally hired by women who don't want their husbands to know they've hired me. If we were working in the husband's family home, and there were certain things that he maintained a life connection to, be it a piece of furniture or the spirit of his dead father, I would consider it unethical to try to break his connections without his permission.

No deep psychic work can occur without permission, and I generally consider myself to have a pretty high security clearance, but disturbing people's relationships without their knowledge or consent is more than impolite. When there are situations that involve multiple parties, as say in a divorce or death, it may be fine to remove the old pattern of family energy and its connection to the former spouse, but not alter their connection to their own children.

Dealing With *My Own* Doubts

When I was near to graduating from college, in the mid-90's, my parents came to visit me, and we had a lovely walk in Golden Gate Park. They were proud that I had finally completed the academic achievement they had always expected of me (although my degree was in my self-styled major of Psycho-Spiritual Healing rather than law), and they asked me what I thought I would do for a career. I told them, "Well, the psychic housework has been going pretty well, I've actually been earning a living doing it."

The conversation sort of stopped, and we walked a couple blocks before it resumed. I realized that of all the things that

I had done that hadn't met my parents' expectations, the completely bizarre notion of some metaphysical practice being a career was so outside their frame of reference that they would have preferred that I was a *drug dealer!* Market forces and commodity values were so much more comprehensible to them, and they just couldn't see beyond their own *(somewhat rigidly)* rational framework of reality.

My work and what it makes me is something of a conversation stopper. Either people stop what they're talking about to quiz me about it, or they stop talking to me altogether. From my own rationalist perspective, I can totally appreciate some people's abject refusal to accept what I do, and their need to categorize me as *a whacko!* Once engaged in the discussion, however, I find it be rather entertaining to see them display their own difficulty with reason and logic.

I had a couple houses to heal in LA and went down a day early to visit a friend of mine. Both he and his wife have their master's degrees in science, and he runs a successful business. I arrived in the late afternoon and wound up in the kitchen, where I did what I could to help Lisa prep things. Being tremendous foodies, they had a fabulous dinner planned. We began talking about things, family, life, and eventually my work. Lisa was very interested in what I did, and extremely skeptical.

When Craig arrived, we popped a bottle of wine (which I refrained from, heading into two days of meditation) and the conversation got a little looser. Lisa began to really needle me about how I could possibly believe in energetic forces that were immeasurable by contemporary physics, and I could only relate it to the type of physics that had been researched, and point to the more current research indicating the existence of a number of psi phenomena, of which she had no knowledge. Craig was concerned that she was offending me, but there is nothing I enjoy more than spirited debate, and on we went.

Lisa suggested that perhaps I was working a scam on the mentally deficient, those who believed in "ghosts" and such, so I had to inform her that my clients were normal, average people in all walks of life and that many of them were quite successful in their fields. They didn't all have "ghosts," they just happened to feel uncomfortable things where (and only where) they lived. More wine ensued, and Lisa contended that I might be using some hypnotic power, that made people think that I had done something to their house, when I had really just made them overcome their problem thought pattern.

While I appreciated the suggestion that I was truly Svengali-like (able to hypnotize complete strangers at a glance and repair their malfunctioning psyches), I had to laugh out loud. "Which one of us sounds insane, now?" I asked her. "You're suggesting that people would track me down, *from out of nowhere,* to fix their house, and then, having only spoken to me for an initial phone call, that I would be able to cast a spell over them that made all their problems go away? If that were the case, *why would I bother with houses?* **I could just have anyone I wanted writing me checks, and hang out at the beach!"** Well, that ended that conversation, although dinner was lovely.

Still, it's just not "normal" to do what I do, and despite the previous several chapters, I find it hard to describe what I do without sounding more than a tad bit weird. A friend from high school once asked me, "What do you do when you go to someone's house, really?" I knew I couldn't explain it to him, so I said, "I sit around, act like I'm meditating for a couple hours, after which my client often serves me lunch. We hang out, talk, and then I go back to work. I wander around the house until eventually, I take a big dump! That makes me feel so much better that I guess the house feels better too! Then the client writes me a check and I split." We had a good laugh, but honestly, I had no idea what to tell him. It's challenging *to me* to believe that I actually *do* what I do.

There are times I get a little bit paranoid; "If all this is really happening, in this arena that is so culturally denied, how is it that *I've* been empowered to do this work? Yikes! What *does* that make me?" I like calling myself a metaphysician, but it doesn't take too much reminding to be humble about it. Fortunately, the work itself has nothing to do with me, other than the fact that I have the skills. Healing someone's house forces me to step *out* of my internal world and up to a higher level of perception, focus, and capacity to manipulate energy. What keeps humbling me is my clients' frequently awed, and sometimes ecstatic response to the new feeling of their house, and what that really means, in terms of the nature of the reality we all share.

Part II

The Houses

Family Business

FIRST AND FOREMOST IN MY line of work are the connections within families. Obviously, these are the ties that bind us; to place, history, and each other. Our desire to recall the simple days of our youth, our connection to our parents, or our love for a partner or children can become a great yearning as we approach death. And when there are unresolved issues burdening us, it makes it all the more difficult to leave our bodies behind.

Before we approach the end game, however, we may have opportunities to resolve the issues we have with our parents, because those are at the root of our lives. We all have to deal with our parents, *and* with their deaths. Except for the rare cases where we die first, leaving unfinished business, then it becomes a job for me.

Deb Jacobs called me to help her expedite the sale of her mother's house, which was being held up by complications with her step father. By the time I arrived on scene the sale of the house had dragged on for a year, while Deb's stepfather played power games with her, dangling the house and her inheritance rather than supporting her through the painful transition of relinquishing a family home filled with memories.

The house itself was nautically themed, sitting right on the bay in Tiburon, with an almost lighthouse shaped exterior, porthole windows, and rigging hardware within. The first sense I got from it was longing, as if the house itself was keeping lookout for a lost ship. It reminded me of Gull Cottage, from *The Ghost and Mrs. Muir.*

Deb's mother, Roma Jean, had died after a fairly long bout with cancer, and while her physical pain was evident, even more so was her longing. Her son, Deb's younger brother, had disappeared some 20 years prior, having vanished without a trace after being diagnosed with a health complication. No one knew what had become of him, *or if he was even alive*, but his mother kept watch, as from a ship's lonely helm, looking out on the bay and waiting for his return for all those years.

This determination left a very palpable sense of her energy, her refusal to give up her ceaseless watch despite the pain that she suffered as the cancer overtook her body. Deb had a sense of it, but had tried her best to ignore it. The thing that pushed her into calling me was that her dog, Bailey (a very friendly yellow Lab), refused to enter the house. While Roma Jean was alive, she was always a little uncomfortable around animals (leaving Bailey to be a little less vivacious around her), but now that she was dead, Bailey would bark and start shaking when approaching the front door, and cry and fuss so much inside the house that Deb would have to put her back in the car to calm down. Bailey's fearful reaction was new and completely out of character.

Roma Jean had been a strong woman with indomitable will. She and her first husband's marriage had been difficult, particularly after the disappearance of Deb's brother, who was the favored child. Roma Jean's intransigence was apparent to me, and the sense of her holding on, holding out, through all of her own suffering, for the never relinquished possibility of her son's return, permeated the house. True to form with that longing, his room had been left fairly intact, as one would keep things while their child went away to college.

I felt that a major part of Roma Jean's attachment was due to feeling that she had, in some respects, driven him off. Whether through smothering or demand for perfection, she had never allowed him to be himself, and had he returned, she would still be unlikely to offer him that freedom. In his absence, however, all the dreams of redemption were hers, and while that dream stayed alive, there was no reason to change her style of parenting in regard to Deb, who bore the brunt of her emotional withering.

As I began clearing the stains of physical pain and death from her bedroom (a major roadblock to begin with), I was struck by her complete investment in the house and intention to remain there on lookout. It appeared to me that the whole house had become connected to her heart, tortured; broken, longing for the lost love she imagined would redeem her. Committed to forlornly waiting, she and the house would not allow themselves to relinquish their posts. Using my own sense of observation, from that vantage point, to inquire about her son's existence, I saw that he was long since dead, but without ever having confirmation of that, could any mother give up hope???

It was a sad situation, but ending her spirit's fantasy, so that she could move on, perhaps to meet him again in another life, was clearly necessary. Fortunately, at the edge of the water, I was able to tap into some considerable nature energy, and opening the gate to the West, I relieved her of her watch.

When I had finished with my work, Deb brought Bailey in for a reality check. Bailey went through all four levels of the house without a hitch, and fell asleep on the living room floor, which had been impossible for the prior year.

But wait there's more!

After the lighthouse sold, which was not long after I cleaned, Deb realized she should have me do her own house, which had energetic debris from a death and some difficulty with the former tenants. She had done a fine job of decorating the house, even hanging some of Roma Jean's fabulous paintings, but the energy was still off.

Deb had been trained at *the Academy*, and one of her odd sensitivities was to those paintings. As I said before, Roma Jean had a commanding presence, and Deb felt that her mother was watching her through them. This feeling became increasingly more intense after she died. Deb wanted me to look into the paintings and see if something was going on within them. It was not the first time I had agreed to investigate an unbelievably bizarre job concept, *even for me,* since by and large, my job *is* unbelievably bizarre.

Roma Jean's paintings were incredibly detailed renderings of gardens and forest paths, so lifelike that you felt as if you could walk into the paintings and be in the places themselves. As I sat in front of each one, I focused myself, and mentally did just that. All of the sudden, I felt as if I was standing in nature, but when I looked behind me, where the room should have been, there was Roma Jean, at her easel. Seemingly, she had painted herself into another world that she could view this one from, and after her death, this was more and more the refuge she could inhabit. It was unlike anything I've ever experienced, psychically or in my appreciation of art, which I have traveled the world to engage in; and startling to me, as I thought that removing her spirit from her house had been the end of the line. I still don't know how or what part of her managed to manifest that way, but having no business disturbing her posthumous existence, I went about sealing off the different paintings, closing the portals that allowed her to look back into this world.

Deb opted not to be at her house while I was working there, and that was fine. Some of my clients, particularly those who are engaged in this sort of work, like to be around to see how it feels, but many prefer not to, and I can certainly understand why. Returning to the house, she felt it had changed entirely, and looking at the paintings, she was no longer being affected on an energy level or feeling ill-at-ease with them.

The funny thing about that job was that Deb asked me to stay for dinner and meet her neighbor, Jan. Jan showed me her house, which she had purchased almost two years prior. The main bedroom, which she had planned to move into when she bought it, was full of boxes that she had still not unpacked. She slept in the "spare room." She had known that a prior owner had committed suicide in the house, but, being a rational woman, thought nothing of it. She still liked to think that she had simply decided not to use that room. While I could respect her desire to think that, I found it interesting that she hadn't considered the incongruousness of the fact that she was using a quarter million dollars worth of her real estate as a storage space, or that she hadn't ever opened her boxes once they had been relegated to that room.

A House Divided

Dia North called me to clean her house, which had been in her husband Don's family for over fifty years. Don and his twin brother Dan had inherited the house after their mother was murdered in a carjacking incident. After much wrangling over ownership and living arrangements, Dia and her husband took over the property and moved in.

They did an incredible job of remodeling, building a professional kitchen for Don, and an office for Dia's business, painstakingly coordinating interiors and planting a wonderful garden, but there was still a feeling of great sadness in the house, and continued tribulation over family squabbles. You see, Dan and his wife had moved in originally, but were unable to buy Don's half of house, so Don and Dia bought them out. This caused a major rift in the twins' relationship, and a very spiteful feeling from Dan's wife, Tina, toward Dia. With this constant negativity focused on and around them, it was easy to see how Dia and Don were starting to feel bad about the whole thing.

As the most recent tenants, Dan and Tina's energy was the top level to be cleared, but it wasn't as if they were just some renters. They had an intimate relationship with the house and its history, as well as tremendous anger over leaving. While the impact of dead people on a house can be quite powerful, the feeling of someone whose conscious energy is focused on you, through their own intimate connection to your space, is hard to ignore.

This was the first time I worked in a house that had been the childhood home of the current owners, and I saw how that connection made for deeply rooted residual energy. This was amplified by the fact that the twins had such a close relationship and rivalry. The division and energetic interference between them was clearly perceptible to me, and while (as men) they may have ignored it, it was clearly playing out in the power struggle for ownership. Tina too plugged into the rivalry, and was extremely bitter about having to leave. Having worked for Dia's business, she was able to worm herself further into the situation by filing a groundless lawsuit against her. Dia was now running her business out of her lovely basement office, but felt mired in stuck energy and overwhelmed by Tina's attacks.

She was also unwittingly faced with the task of stepping into unfillable shoes. Don's mother was not only the matriarch of the house, but of the entire extended family and probably that section of the city, and her untimely death left quite an impact. At the first Christmas that Dia took up the duty of hostess, amidst multiple generations of the family, what had traditionally been a "stay up until four, sleep on the floor" event wound up in a brawl that everyone left by ten. Of course, Dia *could not be her mother-in-law,* but that expectation amongst the family set the stage for a disaster.

With the focus from all directions on Don's mother and her presence, Dia found it very difficult to be herself in present time. When the time came for me to work with Don's mother, sitting on her antique bed and looking at her chest of drawers (they had kept her furniture), I could feel her energy quite easily. Looking deeper I was immediately transported to her car, stopped at a light, as she was being accosted by some young hoodlums. They demanded she get out and leave the keys. Being a stately old dame, she refused, and so they shot her, pulled her out of the car and drove away. I stayed with her there, on the pavement, assisting her death, again and again, working to separate her from the violently charged energy of that incident, and from there to dissolve her *desire to hold on to life* from her imbedded connections, through the house, to her history there, and everyone connected to it. (It was a lot to experience, *and to keep track of.*)

Once that was done I was able to renegotiate the contracts,

as everyone involved had some level of relationship to her, which was primary to their relationship to the house. The presence of Don and Dan's life history also needed clearing, as it acted as a constant reminder of their conflict. Their childhood room (which Dia could not figure out *what* to do with, other than take a nap) had become a battle ground of memories, through which they were inseparably connected to each other, in their current antagonistic relationship.

This was one of the first jobs that I did for a client who paid for it herself, unbeknownst to her husband, who was not particularly aware of his own energetic position in the scheme of things or thusly committed to resolving them. In some respects, I may have overstepped some ethical boundaries before I knew they existed, but there was a clear connection between all of the parties and my client, who needed to have things resolved. When I checked in with her later that week, she told me that when Don had come home that day, he had asked her what she had done to the house, expecting that the new feeling was the result of one of her many interior design touches. When she laughed an "Oh nothing," he suggested that perhaps he'd rather not know.

When the next holiday season came around, and Dia elected to have their holiday dinner again, there was no fighting, trauma or anger at the fact that she was not the family matriarch. Everyone was able to have a splendid time, and stayed all night, because they were able to settle into who they were at that moment, not who they were in relationship to their family history.

Listening To Spirits

IT'S NOT OFTEN THAT WE give ourselves permission to listen to spirits. As children, yes, although we're likely to have given that up with age. For most of us, the cultural parameters that define who we are don't allow for such *nonsense*, and our belief thereby limits our perception. If spirits were actually trying to tell us something, would we be able to understand it? Or would we simply deny that it happened? For some people, it's not as easy to ignore, and when faced with a clear communication, the only answer is to listen up.

Maid Service

My friend Raul was visiting his girlfriend in Miami, and somehow got to talking about ghosts. As it turned out, her best friend had a serious house problem, which led me to a very interesting job. Mia's house was built in 1903 by an original developer of what is now the city of Miami. It was a beautiful mansion, with lovely grounds, and it became the long time residence of Coconut Grove's mayor. Shortly after moving in, Mia and her husband did tremendous renovations, building a whole new upper wing, with a master suite, so there was plenty of room.

Mia brought her maid and cook with her to the new house, and had them move into the downstairs bedrooms, as these older Cuban women were really a part of her family. Before long, however, they refused to live there, moving out back to the old servant's quarters, because they were beset by the spirit of a woman who bothered them. She hovered around them in the kitchen and dining room as well, making them feel their work was always being inspected. Out back they could at least *sleep* in peace.

Mia found this somewhat upsetting, as did her husband, who

was an extremely rational businessman. It was as if a family member had decided to move out to the garage, all for some crazy superstition. Mia herself had felt uncomfortable in the old master bedroom, however, heard clunking footsteps going downstairs at three a.m. and occasionally the sound of the doorknob turning back and forth. She even saw the TV flicker to life, but somehow refused to believe it was happening. While her bedroom was uncomfortable to be in, and, by her own admission, "impossible to sleep in," the fact that these old Cuban women saw apparitions was over the line. So they chalked it up to cultural differences. It wasn't the sort of problem she could really address, and after moving into the new master suite, she put it out of her mind.

Meanwhile, Mia's eldest daughter, Teresa, moved into the old master suite for her last year of high school. While she too refused to believe in ghosts, by the time she went off to college she had developed a sleep disorder, which no one thought to blame on the disturbance. It wasn't until she was home for spring break that she had a recognizable encounter. She was up at three a.m. for an early morning flight, when her bedroom door came ajar, revealing an iridescent human figure. Teresa was shaken, but managed to make her flight, and told her mother about it on the phone that night. She described it as being neither opaque nor translucent, with shimmering colors radiating from its shoulders. When Mia shared the story with the maid she replied, "Yes, it is a shawl she wears around her shoulders."

When this happened the maids told Mia of other strange occurrences; televisions turning on suddenly, noises in Teresa's empty room, and how her bed would appear on some mornings to have been slept in. After Mia discussed this with Raul, and he told her about what I do, she broached the topic with her husband. I'm not sure whether he feared losing his rationality or if it brought up some spiritual dilemma for him, but he adamantly refused to allow any such thing to go on in "his" house. Perhaps he had also been aware of the problem, and was afraid of concretizing it.

In either case, part of my job was to get there late enough in the morning and be gone early enough that he couldn't possibly be home from work. It wasn't the first time that man's indifference or insensitivity to (or underlying fear of) the energetic realm has shaded the nature of my work, but it certainly was the most intense declaration. Fortunately, Mia was a successful business woman in her own right, so she felt free to ignore her husband's control orientation. It gave the job an extra spy-like twist for me, too, which I appreciated.

As I toured the house it came to me that what made it so difficult for Mia and her husband to understand what was going on was that the two of them were completely separated from the rest of the house. The master suite they had built was incredibly spacious, with an entertainment center and lounging area, dual bathrooms with dressing rooms, right out of *Architectural Digest*. It became the place they spent most of their time. It extended off the upper level of the house, and with the maids doing all the cooking and such, Mia and her husband really only had to come down for meals, to go to work, or to entertain.

Being built in the last decade, it appeared to me that their bedroom had been outside of the spirit's realm. Even for Mia, the spirit didn't exist. She told me that she had never seen it. But it was clear that *something* was happening, and I realized (having worked on homes that have been moved or had additions made to them) that this spirit could only exist within the field of the house that it knew, *the house as it had been when* it *lived there.* This made the entire master suite *nonexistent* and inaccessible to it. The old master bedroom, which was now Teresa's, was clearly the living space of this spirit, and it didn't have any trouble making its presence known in there, which is why Mia decided to fly me out.

It was a fairly large job to tackle this estate in the limited time I had, but there were some definite points of focus. I discussed with the maids (in my poor Spanish and their broken English) why they refused to live in the house, the kind of feelings that they had around working there, and the events that had occurred in the house, just to get an experiential idea of what was going on. It seemed that this somewhat aristocratic spirit was checking up on things, methodically overseeing and prodding them, trying to conduct the day's cooking and cleaning and ordering of the house, which is what led me to believe that it was the spirit of the old mayor's wife.

Fortunately for me, the three hundred year old Oak tree in the backyard gave me an incredible grounding anchor from which to meditate and conduct earth energy throughout the house. I had to melt down and reset the entire structure so that the newer sections were contiguously grounded with the older, and to clear and flush all of the incredible history out of the building. I moved into the original master suite to trace and erase all of Mrs. Mayor's intention to oversee her dominion, and from there could escort her trapped spirit to the ocean, and beyond.

It was pushing four o'clock when I finally got done with the house, but I had time to check in with the maids, whom I had to respect as coming from a culture with far more spiritual awareness than my own. They told me that they felt a profound change, and thanked me profusely for my work, which I was able to complete (and make my exit) before the return of Mia's doubting husband, whom I'm sure wondered why things felt so much calmer after I had left.

In speaking with Mia to clarify this chapter, she wrote me — "Years later, I would recall how tense I was before we moved in to the house. I was having dreams that the house was haunted. I dreamt that there existed, in a non-accessible attic, a whole family of ghosts. In my dream — I would open a door and would discover a hidden upstairs floor full of empty rooms. When we did the renovation I began to dream again that there were ghosts in the underlying structure of the house. And I remember thinking 'I hope this construction' clears it of them. In fact, it wasn't until after the construction that weird things really began to happen."

It amazes me to find that she had had such clarity about what was going on, but had somehow managed to push it out of her mind by the time she called me. How clear our vision is in dreams, where the layers of what we're allowed to think can't stop us from seeing what truly is.

Visionary Artist

A musician friend of mine called to ask if he could refer me to his girlfriend, who was having some problems with her home. "Of course!" I told him, "How else do you think she'd find out about me? *Magic?*" So he did, and Jennifer called me. She had become very concerned over the fact that her four-year-old daughter, Delilah, kept having nightmares from which she would awaken crying.

This had never been the case before they moved into their new house, and these nightmares were thematically consistent. There was an old woman standing at the foot of her bed, beckoning her, frighteningly. Jennifer would go into Delilah's room and explain to her, "there's no woman here, honey," but Delilah would refuse to return and fearfully demand entry to her mother's bed.

In addition to the old woman, Delilah would hear whispering, giggling, and sometimes arguing in her room. She also saw a boy whom she called Daeken, who was blue and would trip her as she ran along through the hallway or in her room. Jennifer told me, "I was watching a couple of times, and it was as if she ran into an invisible log and then tumbled over it, sprawling out on the floor, very surprised."

These things had definitely become bothersome, but more recently there had been some events that shocked her into calling me, primarily, her daughter's uncanny predictive abilities.

They kept a pet bunny in a cage in the back yard, which Delilah liked to paint pictures of. She painted dozens of pictures of it, but they began to included the words "SATAN", "DEMON" and "MORT," although at age four, she couldn't really write or spell and had never heard them before. Jennifer told me, "It was really weird, because I don't believe in Satan, or that such a being has any power except in our imaginations, but somehow that was the scariest word that she wrote."

One afternoon Delilah asked her, "Mommy, can we get a new bunny after Snowflake dies?" Jennifer was somewhat taken aback, but, since there was no reason for the rabbit to die, replied, "Well, sure, honey, but Snowflake's fine, she's not going to die."

"Okay," said Delilah, who left that day to spend the weekend with her father. While she was away, however, two Rottweilers running loose in the neighborhood worked through a hole in the fence, got into the rabbit hutch, and tore the rabbit to shreds.

Jennifer was terrified by this, and avoided broaching the subject when Delilah returned. Delilah however, went straight into her easel and created a painting of her rabbit covered in bloody red Xs with the words "RED RUM," written across the top. When she showed Jennifer the picture she added narration, saying "they hit him here, and here, and here," pointing to the red X's. Jennifer showed me this painting and it was stunning. It was clear that she was communicating with something outside of her own highest capacity. So I went to work.

The house had been transplanted by the owner, who rescued it from decrepitude in a lesser neighborhood of Oakland by jacking it up and moving it to Berkeley for refurbishing, thereby filling his vacant lot and improving the structure's property value in one fell swoop. But in this process the grounding of the house was completely severed. The whole structure was transplanted to a place where it had no connection.

I took a Feng Shui perspective to think about this. Feng Shui is based on orientation to the compass points, to the flow of energy in relationship to those compass points, and how the earth's rotation shifts the direction of certain energies over periods of time. The energy coming toward and through a house changes over time, but while the main facing of a house may be changed to adjust for this, the house still sits where it sits.

Much like a Joshua Tree can't be transplanted without consistent 360 degree alignment to the earth, it seems that a house doesn't fare well being moved either. What I found looking at this house was that because of its new compass alignment, it could no longer naturally ground, it was both off the magnetic alignment to which it had been built, and the earth itself.

Consequently, the spirit of the elderly woman, who had lived in the house for decades and died there while it was in Oakland, stayed there, inhabiting her lovely bedroom with the French doors onto the garden, which was now Delilah's. She was *stuck* there, unable to leave, having been transplanted along with the house, which had fallen into disrepair while sitting in Oakland. With her house being set on a different position on the magnetic grid, her move to Berkeley offered her no capacity to orient herself to the possibility of leaving. Confused as the sun rose and set in the wrong windows, she demanded connection with whomever was nearest (both in the human and apparently the entity realms), to help her out.

Unfortunately for Delilah, that happened to be her, and as a four year old she didn't have a lot of capacity to extract herself from the situation. She was wide open, much too young to have built up any psychic defenses or to rationalize away what she was experiencing. This was clear to me, and I took it seriously. Trapped spirits are one thing, clients who are suffering from the effects of living with them are another, but kids who are sucked into the line of fire ***really*** need my help.

The first biggest step was to figure out how to reset the contract with the house to allow it to adapt to its new magnetic alignment, twisting its etheric blueprint to align to the grid in Berkeley; but after that, the work came into focus. Delilah's death painting showed me that she was becoming connected to some kind of entity, which was causing her violent precognition and perhaps manifesting the event as well. Perhaps this entity was also Daeken, I didn't ask its name. Clearly, however, I needed to pay particular attention to removing it.

This entity energy had piggybacked in on the spirit of the old woman, whose fear of death had forced her to remain, and whose lovely domain made it seem all right. Her presence may have contributed to the demise of the house while in Oakland, but finding herself really trapped after the building was moved, she sought contact with anyone available. After disconnecting the entity, all I needed to do to release her spirit was show her the door, and the room suddenly returned to an expansive feeling of opening to a garden.

Jennifer told me that Delilah slept in her room that night, and thereafter, without awakening from any nightmares or to any presences. She also stopped talking about Daeken, the old lady, and the whispering, giggling voices. Perhaps best of all, her artwork took a distinct turn from violently precognitive to playfully childlike.

Sell or Hold

ABOUT A THIRD OF MY work is in homes that my clients are trying to sell. They don't know why, but the places just sit on the market. Sometimes they're showcase homes, sometimes not, but it's always puzzling, that every deal falls through, or no one even makes an offer. Having lived there so long, my clients lack the ability to see what might be uncomfortable to a potential buyer, especially when they've already swept them under the rug.

Hey Pops

Bill and Lara were close friends of my friends Tim and Randi, and I had met them socially several times. On occasion, conversation dipped into my work, but after they decided to move, Randi suggested they hire me. Of course, they didn't. They had a beautiful hilltop house in Marin, full of Bill's exquisite handmade cabinetry, and the market was booming.

Bill had planned to roll his Marin house into a rural property where he could build a custom house and have his shop adjoining it. He had already bought the property and eventually broken ground, but in the year they'd been trying to sell the house nothing happened. They'd been through a change of listing and realtor; they'd had numerous open houses, showings, and some interest, but nothing panned out. This was extremely odd for Marin (where you could sell an outhouse in a junkyard for half a million), and they were beginning to get a little desperate. They had already begun settling up their business affairs in Marin and needed dough to build their new house.

I talked to them occasionally over the period of that year, running into them at events at our friend's house, and offered them my services when nudged by Randi, but "no, no, it was nothing out of the ordinary." They just assumed it was taking a long time and they couldn't really imagine why there would be any sort of problem like the ones that would require my attention. Eventually, because at this point it was starting to really cost them, they decided — what the hell. I offered them easy terms, based on the sale of their house, so they didn't really have anything to lose. Still though, when I spoke to them they didn't really have any idea why there might be a problem. They didn't know the previous owner very well, but they had been there over a decade so there didn't seem to be any residue from that, or any problem that they could put their finger on.

Timing being what it is, they weren't quite able to get my form filled out and back to me until I'd gone over to the house to meet them and do the job. It certainly was a lovely home, tucked up on the hill with glass running the east wall looking down on the bay, so I looked through the rooms and then talked to Lara about the situation. She told me that the downstairs section of the house, which was now somewhat vacant, doubled as an in-law unit, and had been home to Bill's father for the last few years of his life.

They were very close; the whole family. Bill and Lara's sons spent a lot of time doing things with their grandfather and they all lived there together for several years. Quite unexpectedly, some eighteen months prior, Bill's father had succumbed to a heart attack, right there in the downstairs. Bill had found him there, and that was a great loss for them all. Perhaps that spurred their decision to move. It rather amazed me, that in a year of talking to me about my line of work, it hadn't come up at all, but I know it's hard to convert from a rational perspective to seeing things the way I do, or recognize the signs when they're that close.

I could tell that Lara was feeling a bit affected by opening this memory, and I asked her if there had been any occurrences that might have indicated to her that Bill's father was still there. She mentioned that she had in fact seen him walking through the house, and setting the dinner table once, as he always did, but in the twilight of the evening she had dismissed these spectral appearances as tricks of the light.

Whenever there's a deep emotional connection to a person and their death, it doesn't so much matter whether the person who has died is really leaving a *ghost*. The intense energetic tie the living and the *memory* of the dead, and the expectation of them to simply walk back into life, holds their energy in such a way that their place is marked. For Bill and Lara, trying to sell the house and leave that chapter behind, *without having fully let go or completed their grieving for his father*, still kept a very large piece of him in residence downstairs.

While it's always up to each of us to complete our own process, bidding adieu to Bill's father, clearing the whole family's energetic connection to their past together, and dissolving their expectation of seeing Bill's father again among the living, became my job. It was easy enough to feel him downstairs, and sense the way he fit into the family rhythm, with the boys joining him to watch TV or him coming upstairs to help out at mealtimes. It was the love of being a family, and his family's love for him, that kept him there, and without ever wanting to let go, or being able to properly say goodbye, they held together.

The boys had moved out in that time, though, and Bill and Lara needed to as well. Bill's father understood that, and when offered this chance to move on, he gladly met with the light. With the house cleared and reset for their greatest capacity to move on in life, it was only two weeks before Bill and Lara had an offer on the house that allowed them to move into their future.

Joker that I am, I chided them later about how much their rational perspective had held them back.

Nature At Work

THE EARLIEST RELIGIONS, AND MANY that still exist, bear witness to the power(s) of nature, and the unique spirit family that inhabits our world. While we do our best to ignore them, mercilessly extracting every useful substance discovered as we pave and pollute the planet, nature, in all her forms, continues to speak to us. Using elemental energy the way I do, I'm frequently made aware of the dissonance in our relationship, but sometimes that awareness is made extremely acute.

Bird's Eye View

Diana Willard called me after her housemate Cathy recommended me. I had worked on Cathy's daughter's house, and she had heard about the good results, so she hoped I might be able to help them too. The problem with Diana's house was that it was being attacked by birds, in two specific, different ways. On the right side of the house it was being attacked by a robin, and on the left, by a flock of nuthatches. I had never heard of anything like this, but I hadn't heard of anything else I was working on, so I made the appointment and drove over to El Cerrito to meet them.

The house had been a two bedroom ranch style, but the family that owned it had built additions off the back wall. Each addition was built like a half "A" frame, sticking off the back of the house, with the empty gap in the middle forming a patio space. The half As were angling up off the house, like the fins on the space shuttle, so the high wall was in the back. Those walls had windows facing into a field, and those were the ones that the birds flew into.

On the right side of the house, starting at dawn, a robin would fly into the window, very hard, wham! Then it would flutter its way up the window, wings brushing against the glass, fluflfuflfuflfuf, and then fly away. It would repeat the process every fifteen or twenty minutes until the late morning. On the left side of the house, the nuthatches nesting in neighboring trees would fly in groups against the window, *flapthumpthumpflapthumpthumpthump* bounce off and fall into the dirt, and fly away, only to repeat some variation of the process throughout the early morning.

Diana occupied the left back room and Cathy the right. There was a bedroom inside the house which Diana had taken originally, but it proved to be uncomfortable for her, so she turned it into a guest room. I thought that odd, considering that her room was under attack every morning, but she wasn't the only one. All of her guests found it uncomfortable as well, and migrated to the couch in the living room to sleep.

The house backed against an open field, and Diana told me that when the additions were built, the owners had taken down a very large tree, which had been home to many of these birds. The stump of it was still apparent at the edge of the patio, between the two rooms. In addition to its metaphysical problem, the house had a cracked water line underneath it, which caused constant seepage through the front yard and out into the gutter. The water company had scoped it, but it was going to be a major job to dig under the house to repair it, so they left it as it was.

I sat down in the back room and tried to extend my consciousness into what had been there before, to see why the birds kept coming back. Apparently, the tree which had been cut down was a tremendous social hub, a home and feeding ground for many birds and animals. The homing sense of these particular birds brought them back continually from the other trees out in the field, to what I could only describe as the phantom imprint of that tree. They were returning home, except that home wasn't there anymore.

What was really weird was that in turning my senses outward, to see what the birds were looking for when flying into the windows, and whether they were expressing some particular anger or frustration, was that they were doing no such thing. They were looking for water! Somehow, the back rooms, with their odd shapes and windows, appeared to these birds to be tunnels leading down to the water that they could sense running beneath the house.

My job, in essence, became dissolving the phantom appearance of the tree, and its historic relationship to the blueprint of the house, so that the birds were no longer attracted to what had been gone for several years already. Since they had little grounding of their own, and no real connection to the grounding of the house, I also had to connect the additions to the house and expand its grounding to encompass them. After that they weren't looking like tunnels into the underground water supply but sealed parts of the house, which made a tremendous difference.

Moving into the main part of the house and sitting in the vacant guestroom, I was met by the unbearable sadness and oppressed feeling of a teenage boy, whom I came to believe was being abused, either emotionally or physically, by his father. It didn't seem that he had a particularly defiant streak, but perhaps he was not satisfying his father, who felt to me to be high in expectation and quick to anger.

The boy's long standing malaise, in his torturous paternal relationship, had left an imprint in the walls that was stifling. The room felt so constricting that it was difficult to breathe. I could see why guests would feel uncomfortable here, and why my client couldn't use it herself. It was oppressive, threatening, and it required that I reach back into the history of the house and their family to dissolve their remnant energy.

This was fairly early in my career, so I couldn't offer any guarantee that my work would stick, or even be effective. Everything I did at this point was an experiment that tested my intuitive grasp of the forces at work, my ability to design a methodology, on the fly, and my capacity as an energy practitioner to implement it and resolve the situation. It was beyond my expectation to have really fixed things, but when I spoke to Diana over the ensuing months, there were no more avian assaults on the house, she began to felt much better, and over time, people stayed in the guestroom.

A Boy Loves a Tree

When Elizabeth called me, she was in her first year at *the Academy* and had already attempted to get a group of her classmates together to work on her house. I don't know if they ever made it, or knew what they were looking for, but fortunately, she was working with another intuitive consultant who recommended me. The main problem that she saw with her house was that the 60-year-old oak tree in the backyard was dying an unpleasant death. Its trunk was populated by strange boils, and whereas the tree was putting out new shoots for spring, nearly half of them were brown and withered, dead on arrival. It was a situation that the previous owners had tried to remedy by calling the city, whose arborists had done some kind of tree surgery, cutting open the trunk and pouring chemicals into it, which left a gaping rent that had never healed. Still, no one had been able to properly diagnose what was wrong, and the tree appeared to be succumbing.

It was quite a large tree, at least 35 feet tall with a canopy that stretched the entire span of the back yard. While it would have been quite expensive to remove (or worse, let fall into the house), what Elizabeth said about it was much more telling. "I really just love having this tree in my yard. It's a beautiful tree and makes my backyard special. The whole character of my yard and the view from all its windows would change without it. This tree is special." Kay, the intuitive who had referred me, told Elizabeth that the energetic problem with the tree was also leaching over into her lemon tree, which seemed to be getting the disease, and had started producing bizarrely deformed lemons.

I was a little bit reticent to take this job, because I certainly couldn't promise to heal Elizabeth's tree. I do pretty well with living things, but my focus is on inanimate structures, and the effects of the no longer living. While I *know* what I *can* do, however, I *don't* really know what I *can't,* and I figured it was worth taking a look at. When I tried to probe a little further into the condition of the house, Elizabeth told me she thought the house was fine and was only concerned with the tree, or perhaps that having me do both would be too expensive. I'm pretty clear about the fact that if somebody calls me there's got to be something going on with their house, so I told her I would come do her house, then see what I could do about the tree, as an offering.

On my questionnaire Elizabeth stated that her daughter had a lot of difficulty sleeping in her room, had nightmares and often woke upset, which is an indication to me that there's something going on. I particularly question my clients about the experiences, responses, beliefs, and emotional patterns of their children in reference to what might be happening in their house, and her daughter's behavior indicated something to me.

Elizabeth's neighbors, whom she found rather unpleasant, were quite forthcoming, having lived there for fifty years themselves. They gave her a detailed history of the house, and something of the emotional situation going on there with the previous owners, the Sterlings. This information gave me an inkling of what might be happening, which was confirmed when I began to work in Elizabeth's daughter's bedroom. Here I was confronted by the spirit of Brian, the son of the Sterlings, who had chosen to remain in this, his only home, in a relationship that no one else had suspected.

Brian had forged an alliance from early childhood with the oak tree, which his father planted as an acorn, found on a nature walk soon after moving there in 1940. While Brian was still fairly young, his father died, and perhaps this is what made him connect so intensely with the tree, *it held something of his relationship with his father.* It took up the entire expanse of his bedroom window, and I believe that the tree became Brian's closest friend, while living there, almost in its canopy. He spent hours and days and weeks climbing it, and years looking into it from his window - watching the shoots burst into leaves in spring, then flutter down in autumn, leaving the bare trunk slicked with winter rain — saw the doves build nests, then hatch and feed their young — being so connected to this plant life form that I could feel their deep emotional bond still reaching from the bedroom into its core. (A relational pattern, I might add, that Elizabeth had stumbled right into.)

Mr. Sterling's death created a difficult emotional dynamic for Brian and his mother, forcing each to become what they both now lacked. Perhaps she had smothered him, sheltered him longer than necessary, or needed more than he could give her. Perhaps her overarching control prevented him from developing outside relationships, making the tree his only escape. It's hard to say how that played out, exactly, but over time, Mrs. Sterling developed diabetes, which diminished her sight and limited her mobility, so Brian wound up caretaking her, becoming a stay-at-home adult son. I think this loss of freedom caused him a certain level of resentment, and Brian began to drink.

He drank, perhaps secretly, in his bedroom, and felt his connection with the tree. All of his boyhood visions, his sense of wonder and connection to nature, the freedom and expansiveness of sitting perched in that tree, churned up resentment; for his loss, his undesired responsibility, and his inability to create his own life or seek his own freedom. As the years went by, and the bitterness within him grew, he lived his solitary life there, and drank more, perhaps becoming more estranged from and neglectful of his mother, who was now fully in his care.

I can only imagine that she began to resent his behavior as well, because when she died, she left a will that forced Brian to sell the house and keep nothing more than a stipend. Moving into an apartment, away from his lifelong home and only friend, it didn't take him long to drink himself to death, and the tree, which was in emotional congruity with him, began to die as well.

It was a sad situation, so I did my work on the house, relieving Brian's spiritual malaise, his connection with the tree, *and with his mother*, whose remnant energy necessitated some sweeping in other rooms. When I was done with everything in the house, I went out to the yard to see what I might be able to do for the tree. I tried to maintain some sense of discretion, knowing that the unpleasant neighbors might observe me (which they did, leaving some explaining for my client to do), but it was such an amazing specimen that there was really no choice for me but to climb to the very top of the canopy and sit at the highest point I could. It was what the job called for, and quite lovely. Looking over the rooftops in all directions, I could see the bay and the hills, but as I meditated down into this tree, I could feel the death energy of its connection with Brian, like a poison rotting it from the inside out.

I tapped into the tree, into its root system and through them into its connection with the earth, which had waned in its sickly state. Vomiting out Brian's toxic love, I re-grounded the tree in a new sense of earth connection, and drew that energy up through the trunk of the tree, into my own being. Seizing this amazing opportunity, I channeled my awareness through every limb of the tree, out every branch to every leaf, consciously feeling the sunlight on the leaves, electrifyingly converting light into energy through the chlorophyll, pulling that energy through the phloem into the branches, down the trunk, and expanding that energized absorption of sunlight all the way down into the root system, then pulling the mineralized water and earth-grounded connection back up through the xylem, expanding it through the trunk, the branches, and back into each leaf, until I was pulsing through the entire venous structure of this massive oak.

When I ***was*** the tree, I began focusing both forms of energy (and more) into the open wound in the trunk, where the tree surgeons had poured the chemicals. When that felt healed, I attempted to push life back into the 35 or 40 per cent of the branch tips that were brown and dying and dead.

I'd studied tree meditation during my Taoist training, but never dreamt of such a profound expansion of my own perceptual field. I tried to extend that energy across the yard and work with the lemon tree on the same energy level while I was up there, and it came with ease.

I went back into the house and made sure that the work I'd done there was complete, and when Elizabeth returned with her daughters we talked for a bit. She asked about the tree and I told her that I really couldn't say, I had an interesting meditation, but it would be beyond my range of experience to say that it was healed, although I *knew* that her house would feel much different. She sat down on the floor in her daughters' bedroom and concurred then and there that it *did*, which was not what she had expected or even thought about in hiring me.

I called about a month later to check in, and quite to her surprise and happiness, her daughter had now started sleeping through the night with no difficulty. She told me how grounded and clear her house felt, as if a screen had been lifted from it, giving her more space to be herself, to meditate, and to be in her body. On the other hand, there was a new problem. In the month since I had worked there, Elizabeth had found an increasing number of dead squirrels beneath the tree, something she had *never* seen before, and hardly the kind of things she wanted her two and four-year-old daughters to find while playing in the back yard.

Ai yi yi! While my logical mind wondered if some neighbor had started poisoning them, my real worry was that I had inadvertently turned my client's tree into *"the elephants' graveyard."* I told her I'd look at it remotely and returned to the scene in my meditation. I had a chat with the squirrel people, who had been so attracted to the new feel of the tree that they seemed to be honoring it with their deaths. I asked them to go elsewhere to die, which they seemingly agreed to do.

It was over a year later when I spoke with Elizabeth again. She was extremely happy with the change in the house, which, a few months after I left, seem to irritate the irritating neighbor so much that they sold theirs and were replaced by nice people. Amazingly, the oak tree had begun putting out bits of new growth in the deadened areas, and while it hadn't recovered fully, of course, it seemed more vibrant on the whole. She hadn't seen a dead squirrel in a year, and the lemon tree had begun to produce normal lemons!

As I always say, *If life gives you deformed lemons, make deformed lemonade.*

Dreams — Theirs

As I stated before, dreams are a major part of my personal work, and I have had some doozies. But I don't live in my clients' houses. so it's their dreams I'm most interested in. The barrier between worlds is thinnest at night, and the dream plane is open ground, allowing access not only to our subconscious and unconscious minds, but to each others', and to whatever else wants to communicate with us. That's why my clients' dreams are important to me, because in dreams they'll have experiences that their rationality can't deny. They can say that it was only a dream, but the detail and purpose are undeniably real.

Pillow Talk

I had a call from a woman who told me that her dreams were killing her, literally.

Karen had married her boyfriend, who was a widower with three children, whose wife had died a couple of years prior. Karen was a fairly independent artist with her own live/work studio, and before she married her husband he had agreed that when they married they would buy a new home together and start things fresh. After they got married though, he began dragging his feet, and she found that living in her studio was not tenable as a way of starting a family, so she moved into his house. What she experienced there, in her dreams each night, was that her husband's former wife would come to her, stand over the bed, and smother her with a pillow.

Karen would be wrenched from sleep, terrified, gasping for air, only to find her husband asleep, in the dark. Having had that dream numerous times, and fearing for her life and mind, she decided to move back into her studio to sleep, and commute back and forth to deal with her new family. To me, this was less like going back to square one than going back to square minus-one.

Of course, we do what we have to do to stay alive, and Karen couldn't sleep with a murderer. Her predecessor held great interest for me, and in discussing the history of the house, she told me that her husband's widow had been diagnosed with cancer some four years prior, over *two years* before her eventual death. She had gone through the range of treatment options and fought it as long as she could, but was given a fatal diagnosis at about six months. Despite being armed with this knowledge, *she never told her children that she was dying* until a few days before her death.

I can only imagine how difficult it would be to let go of my own children, and how hard I'd fight to deny it happening, but such lapses in communication create deep unspoken bonds. Hers caused such a sudden and intense flare of energy that it was impossible for her to disconnect from her children, and she didn't. She saturated that house, and them. Certainly it was not out of hatred for Karen, but from love for her children, and the inconceivability of letting go of them, that she maintained this connection from beyond. But it was not merely palpable, it was iron-clad, and Karen, in a major sense, stood in the way.

The interesting thing, from the standpoint of my client's dream, was that one of the concessions Karen's husband had made was to replace the bed in which his ex had died, but they put the new bed in exactly the same position. This meant that Karen was essentially sleeping in the spot where X had lingered and died, *and expected to keep inhabiting*, no matter who was *living* there. As her death had been a long time coming, the vibrational stain on the room held her energy there, as if it had been etched in stone.

The other place that her energy was incredibly strong was the kitchen. X was a very committed and dutiful mother, and her presence there, preparing meals, organizing, and structuring her children's days, always made Karen feel uncomfortable; as if she was unwanted, and being physically pushed out. She told me they had purchased a new dining room set when she moved in, but the during first holiday meals she felt as if she was being drilled through as she sat in her chair, at the mother's end of the table.

The other place that was incredibly uncomfortable for her was the library nook. X's energy emanated from every book on the children's bookshelf, imbedded by the hours she had spent reading to her children, and her intention never to be replaced in that role. This intention, *never to be replaced*, imprinted every form of connection to the children, and made it very difficult for Karen to assume the responsibilities of motherhood.

X's connection with her eldest daughter felt the strongest, and her energetic presence in her daughter's room was fairly strong as well, which made another problem clear to me. The children still had strong energetic connections with their mother, even though she was dead. At some level, she was still deeply in contact with them, overseeing them, and that this made it very difficult for Karen to be accepted and form an emotional bond with them. She was the usurper, and that role was unlikely to change while they were still connected to their mother.

This was the first house that brought me to a serious ethical dilemma. While my client had hired me to clear *her* house, so she could live there and make a life for herself and her new family, I did not in any way have permission to alter the energetic agreements between X and her children. I felt that it would have been out of line for me to do so, so I approached things with some finesse. Obviously, the greater impact of X's energetic imprint had to be removed, as her astral visits had become vindictive and could no longer be tolerated. It seemed that her refusal to consciously engage with her impending death had created this situation, so I felt congruent in attending to my client's problem. In retrospect,

I would have had a more compassionate conversation with X, as even now the sadness of her plight strikes me. But that was early in my career, when I felt more capable of simply moving the energy than attending to what it needed.

I did my work to remove her presence, memories, and energetic connections to the bedroom, kitchen, dining room and library, but I allowed X her contracted relationships with her own children. As I explained to Karen, it would be up to the children, when they reached a point of questioning whether it was a healthy energy engagement for *them*, to let go and seek their own healing. I also let her know that X's connection was the major wedge of energy that made it difficult for her to fully bond with the children, and may continue to do so, but that I expected it would be greatly relieved by these changes. While the children could retreat to their own rooms and their private connections to their mother, Karen's position in the home would be secure and comfortable, without fear of reprisals from her husband's widow.

Dreams — Mine

While I don't have to live in my clients' houses, I do travel, and on occasion have a fitful night in an energetically dirty room. I've taken to doing quick cleanings when I'm in suspect hotels *(who knows **what** goes on in there?)*, or staying somewhere for a few days, but never thought to exert the effort when visiting friends, until....

Malpractice

I was talking to my friend Bruce one day, and when the subject of my work came up, he realized I might be able to help his family. His mother-in-law had been trying to sell her house, unsuccessfully. It was actually her second house, a ski chalet in Tahoe, which had been on the market for nearly 18 months. This seemed odd, given the fact that it was certain to be a nice place, so when he asked me to work on it I told him, "Yeah, I'll take a look at it, I have pretty good track record on selling houses."

"Great," he replied, "We can spend a weekend up there, hang out in the snow, have a nice time, it'll be fun."

Bruce, his wife Terry, and I drove up on a Friday evening, had dinner on the way, and got there a little late. We played some cards and talked, but didn't mention anything about the house because it was just *their* house. I didn't know Terry too well, but thought nothing of it. I didn't even have her fill out my questionnaire. It was clearly a nice house, I simply assumed there was some minor problem, which I would resolve. Her mother would be able to sell it, and everything would be fine. After our evening of hanging out, I went to the guest bedroom, contentedly went to sleep, and proceeded to dream.

As I discussed in Section I, throughout my life, and certainly within the history of my psychic training, I have had certain affinity for the dream plane. I have access to information there, *as we all do,* but I have honed my capacity to see things in dreams, even when I'm not looking. Sleeping there that night, I had two dreams.

In the first dream, I was riding BART, the Bay Area rail system, to the new station that they were building at the airport (a project that took 20 years and was still five years from being completed). I arrived at the airport station, but it was just a torn-up construction site, in the middle of nowhere. I got off the train, which departed, and I was left standing in this rubble-strewn lot. Presently, a gang of young hoodlums appeared. They accosted me and began to *kick* my *ass!* Sometimes you have dreams where you have to fight, and can either be capable or incapable, but this was eight guys beating on me. One of them picked up a length of pipe that was laying there and hit me in the lower back, crushing my lumbar spine and paralyzing me on the spot. I lay there on the ground, bloody and in incredible pain, but unable to feel my legs or move them. And then I woke up.

It was still quite late at night, so shook it off and went back to sleep. But before I awoke I had another dream. In this dream I was imprisoned in a mental institution, but it was clear to me that I was completely sane, and that this was some bizarre illusion. The institution itself was like Disney's haunted house, everything was contrived to give the appearance that your senses were lying to you, but it was all so apparently a ruse, so transparent, that it was obvious that I was seeing clearly, and that this fantastic hoax was being foisted on me. A friend of mine was there with me and I told her, "This is not *real.* We are totally sane, and this is all fake. Look! This clock is just running in reverse." But she kept trying to tell me, "No, we're not okay, we have to be here. We're crazy."

"No," I told her. "Just walk out that door. This is all a lie!"

I woke up from that dream in a sweat, and was glad to be back. It was clear to me that something weird was going on in this house, because these were definitely not *my* dreams. I know when I'm dreaming something from my world *(as bizarre as it may be)*, and this clearly was not. These were the dreams of this house, and that made me feel rather uncomfortable. Suspecting that there was something I should know about, I got up, and after some breakfast, carefully broached the subject with Terry.

This house, she told me, was built by her father, a physicist of Swiss extraction, who worked at Lawrence Labs. It was a blueprint duplicate of their house in the Oakland hills, which he had modeled after his grandmother's chalet in Zermatt, where he had spent much of his youth. Growing up in the Alps, his greatest love was skiing. He taught his sons and daughters to ski, and the Tahoe house was very much a part of their life. All until a point at which a ski injury forced him to have surgery on his **lumbar spine!**

Unbeknownst to him, the surgeon made one tiny mistake, slicing into his dorsal nerve root while working in the area around his L5 disc, thus causing irreparable damage. Unbeknownst to *him*, because the hospital opted not to tell him this fact, preferring to hope it would go away. So, while he was recovering from his surgery, he still had tremendous pain in his lower back and legs. His doctors *(don't get me started)* fed him pain relieving drugs, and sleep inducing drugs, and told him that he would soon recover. After some period of time he was still unable to walk properly, and was taking more serious drugs for the pain, but they refused to admit that there was any sort of problem with the surgery that they had performed.

He went on being buffeted about by his health organization, told that the surgery was fine, and that he *couldn't* still be in pain, because he had *had* the surgery and everything was fine. He was referred to a psychiatrist, because he was obviously mentally attached to the idea that he was still in pain. So he went on a regime of psychiatry, being told that his pain was psychosomatic, and that he should take more drugs, both to correct his pain and his improper thinking around the idea that he had pain.

Throughout this time he'd been unable to walk normally, and had turned the downstairs bedroom in his Oakland house into a physical recovery center. He couldn't get up to the second floor of his house, where his bedroom was, so he had his special hospital bed, with lifts and training equipment, all set up in that room. There he could maneuver, recover, and restore his strength, all in the hope of being able to return to the Tahoe house and ski again.

Tired of the pain and the unending process, and certainly of being told he was crazy, he sought a second opinion outside the health organization proffered by his employer. This surgeon revealed to him that he was quite sane, as the first surgery was a serious case of malpractice. They had critically injured him, no doubt, and he would never recover from it, *or be able to ski again!* Once informed of that, he went home to Switzerland, where he took his own life.

The room in which I slept was the matching bedroom to his recovery room at their home in Oakland. Dreaming of being paralyzed and made to think that I was insane, while envisioned through my own framework, were exact models of the situation which he had struggled with for those years up to his taking his own life. An act which *(I needn't bother telling you)* leaves a mark.

With the Tahoe house acting as a mirror for the Oakland house, where her father had spent all that time, in pain, attempting to recover, the job really wound up almost like doing both houses. Separating the whole mirrored effect from the Tahoe house was really a matter of releasing his desire to ski, his boyhood dreams of skiing, and his love of that life for his family. Resetting it for sale was pretty easy. The real work came up in clearing his energy (and the problems that it was causing) from the Oakland house, where Terry's mother still lived. I suppose she had become accustomed to the feeling of her husband's remnant energy, as people do, and had her own and her daughters' emotional debris to wade through all those years. Only the material world issue of selling the Tahoe house gave them any inkling that things could be different.

It was a very interesting job, and of course, the house sold, within a month after I was done. If I had known what I was getting into I might have spent the night in a hotel, but it did teach me to be very careful about sleeping in places before I've worked on them.

Ethics

IN EVERY PROFESSION, PROPER WAYS of doing business are codified and (until recently) abided by. In newer professions, like mine, which had no foundation to build on other than my own integrity and clairvoyant interpretation of the events at hand, codifying ethics has been a procedural development. I've always had to make my decisions on the fly, but I think I show the proper respect.

There *HE* Was

When Debbie Jacobs brought me to work on her mother's house, she was also meeting with Tom, a realtor friend that she was trying to bring in on the listing. After things turned around and she sold the house, he became quite interested in my work. I was equally interested in working with realtors, imagining them to be the golden keys to my market, but as it turns out, realtors have their own job to do and are rarely in a position to employ services such as mine, let alone enter into the sticky discussion of sticky energy dynamics in a property.

Here's why:

A) They can't make decisions regarding the property, only the homeowners can.

B) Selling another expense to the seller risks their relationship, and they don't want my check coming out of theirs.

C) The buyer doesn't want to pay for any more services than they already have to, and imagines that the house is clean.

D) They'd prefer not to know if there *is* an energy problem with the house — the sellers certainly prefer that no one knows, and if the buyer stumbles into it, they can't exactly *prove* anything is wrong.

Tom, however, saw the potential. He was working on a deal

with a widow, Gloria, whose daughter had purchased a house from him and wanted her mother to buy a neighboring property so she could keep her close by and near her grandchildren. The house had already been on the market for six months, but had no offers. Knowing this could flower into an incredible business relationship, I agreed to do the deal on spec, taking my fee only if the house sold.

Tom explained somewhat generally to Gloria what I do and she had agreed to let me work on the place, but I felt a little cautious going in without talking to her about it myself. Most of my clients fill out my questionnaire and talk to me at length about what they sense, and without that I was running blind. I felt my way around for awhile and did some grounding work, but I felt a strong presence of Gloria's husband. She asked me if I'd like some tea, and when we sat down I used that as an opening to get her to tell me about the house and her life there.

She was a calm, courteous, cheerful Brit, and she told me quite placidly how she had emigrated with her husband, after surviving the bombing of London and spending months sleeping in the tube. They had purchased the house upon arriving in California and raised their children there, building on rooms for them and working in the garden that filled the house with splendid blossoms. Her husband had died some five years prior, leaving her well enough off to take care of herself, and while she loved her daughter and grandchildren, it was a bit much to think of moving.

We chatted about various things, without her ever giving any hint that something might be amiss, so I finally had to ask her, "Uhhhh, Gloria, have you seen your husband, here, since his death?" Her composure disintegrated like a bottle hit by a bullet, and she crumpled into a ball of tears. "Right there, coming in the back door from the garden!"

All of the sudden I was in a very odd situation, needing to give her what support I could despite the fact that we were complete strangers. I sat on the couch beside her and put my arm around her, assuring her that it was all right, that I had expected that was true, and that it was obvious they had a very deep connection. She went on to tell me of his occasional appearances over the years, and how much she still missed him.

Now I was faced with a serious dilemma. My agreement with Tom was to get the house to sell, and get paid based on how long that took, but it was clear to me that she was not really ready to let go, and might not *ever* be. Of course, if she didn't, I'd be out a day's work and a potential career making connection, but sitting there with her, the choice of action was obvious.

I told her exactly what my agreement with Tom was, but that if she wasn't ready to move, she could certainly choose to stay there. I asked her if she wanted me to move her husband off to where he belonged, and she agreed that it was time. I finished clearing the house and set it up for her to have the greatest range of possibility, but reminded her that she would have to make the choice about whether or not to leave. The house never sold.

Unfortunately, I was unable to explain the ethical energy dynamics to Tom in a way that made him see past the financial loss, so that relationship never came to fruition, but at least the old widow was happy.

Native Energy

THE NATIVES OF THIS COUNTRY (and native peoples in general) were very respectful of the land, and of their ancestors. But as our development frenzy turns every piece of available land into a potential investment, with no respect for its history or what that might hold, in the places we have defiled we are likely to run afoul of powerful spirits, like…

The Guardian

After Sister Sue sold her house on Mount Tam, she moved her family into a rental and began looking for the *perfect* house. After a few months, she asked me to look into the house she was trying to purchase, because there were a host of contingencies involved in the transaction that were making it difficult. The owners wanted to complete the paperwork and bank transaction by 5 P.M. on a specific date, but the property was only viable for her if she could add a lower floor and build out rooms for her children. The county was taking its sweet time trying to determine whether plans were correct and the permits would be issued, and the escrow on Sue's other house hadn't closed, so she was essentially broke.

As convoluted as it was, I took the job; the non-physical task of trying to energetically negotiate between the owners and their ability to let go of the house, the house itself and its capacity for being altered, the particular inspectors at the county office, and the bank where Sue was waiting for the escrow to close on the sale of her house. Amazingly, on the final day of the window, the county approved the permits at about one o'clock, the escrow closed and the new loan was written at about three o'clock, so by five o'clock the entire transaction was completed. All that remained was for me to clear it out.

It really was incredible, a hexagonal house on a hilltop, with views of Mount Tam, Angel Island and San Francisco from its different thirds, and an open area in the center with a koi pond fed by a water wall. The original owner had developed this entire section of Marin, and built this as his own house, but eventually divorced, moved out, and rented it to an elderly couple. The wife had had a stroke and lived there in a non-ambulatory state for some years. The house held on to this depressed physical sense, but more than that, it felt like it was driving its tenants out. It was hard to conceive of why the original owner would leave such a beautiful house, or why the ensuing occupants would suffer such impairment.

What Sue told me was that in developing this section of Marin during the late '60s, the developer had worked out his back room deals with the county and managed to avoid any archaeological certification. In Denmark, for instance, whenever a building is going to be built, a complete study is undertaken whereby the area is screened off in foot by foot squares and dug by an archeological team to determine whether there are any historical artifacts, before any permission can be given. In California, there are less stringent processes, but laws against disturbing indigenous remains *are* in effect.

This whole section of Marin, like Sue's previous house, and particularly this hilltop, were the domain of the Ohlone Indians, and this point may well have been a burial ground. Whether that's true, or whether it was a point of focused intention for the natives, I'm not sure. But what Sue had found out was that the developer was able to clear the land and essentially bulldoze burial sites, without being shut down or doing any restoration.

While desecration of land itself is developers' meat and potatoes, this was an energetic insult of the highest order.

Since I had such a clear view of Mount Tam, and a well-developed feel for it, I pulled a column of earth energy across to ground myself and the house and got to work. The previous occupants had left a sickly energy, as if the stroke had just been the initial puncture to their auras, which shrank like deflating balloons afterward. The contractor had also been hit, having his dream house life blasted in relationship collapse, from which he limped away. When I got through clearing all of their energy, I began working on grounding the house. I sat out in the back yard, where I could get a feel for the earth, and as soon as I tried to settle down into it, I found myself face to face with a native man. His job, he told me, was to be the guardian of his ancestral burial grounds.

In my practice, I had met with numerous dead spirits and entities, and I had been trained to some degree to work with them. I generally went about my work with a sense of purpose and empowerment. But, when meeting with this native gentleman, my own grounding completely disappeared, and I quickly found myself laying on the ground, spinning, and becoming nauseous, as if I were in a whirlpool. I clutched the ground and held on, with no sense of up or down, and no equilibrium at all. I had come close to this ungrounded feeling once before, in meditation, when I had stepped on an energetic tripwire of my own making, but this was completely overwhelming. It was akin to the worst drunk I'd ever had, and I could tell that if I didn't get it together soon, I would vomit and pass out *(which doesn't look so hot when you're being paid $100 an hour)!*

Obviously, this spirit held the upper hand in our interaction. Time, intention, responsibility and commitment were all in his favor. All I could hope to do was to reestablish my grounding, so I could sit with him, *and respect his honorable position.*

That took **all** of my concentration.

When I did manage to reconnect my first chakra to the earth and sit back up, we engaged in a spirit conversation. The ethical implications of attempting to drive him off for the benefit of my client were clear to me. My work is certainly not about justifying the obliteration of the native populations or the desecration of their land. But that had already occurred, and I expect that those who were instrumental in that unfortunate process had met with energetic reprisals of this guardian's design. No, my job is always about repairing the past, and bringing things into present time, so that was the tack I took.

Much larger than the house or its inhabitants, my job now appeared to be negotiating the fact that in this present moment, there was no returning the land to the stewardship of this guardian. I could only ask permission for my clients to reside in their home, with the intention of making a strong family connection there. Not necessarily in the native way, but conscious and respectful of the beauty of this place, and the passing of his people. I also did what I could to secure the spot as an energy point for his protective overview, and with that agreement, he left me, and the house settled in.

Stain Removal

WHETHER CAUSED BY THE CIRCUMSTANCES surrounding an individual's death, or by their actions while they were alive, stains are literally just that. When we see a stain on a carpet, or a burn mark on wood, we know that wine has been spilled or fire has gotten out of control; so too with energy. If the energy left behind carried a certain feeling and intensity, or actually retains physical properties, I call it a stain. I suppose that almost any of the energy left in a house could be called a stain, but some leave indelible marks.

The Smoking Man

Emily Randall was referred to me by the wife of a reporter who interviewed me for a London newspaper. She was living in an apartment in Redondo Beach, and planning to get married. Her fiancée, Brad, was going to move in with her, and she wanted to clean the apartment out, because she had been living there with a dead guy, whose presence was unmistakable.

Emily woke every morning at 3:13 to the feeling that she was being watched, which, of course, had *never* happened in her previous apartment; neither the waking nor the feeling of being watched. When she would venture out of bed and into the living room, she would smell the pungent odor of someone smoking cigarettes, or even worse, an unemptied ashtray! She looked outside and around the neighboring apartments, but the smell was definitely emanating from her own.

Emily had cleaned the apartment, washed the walls, shampooed the carpet, but it was not the leftover cigarette smell that one finds in old motel rooms. It was a fresh cigarette smell that recurred on a nightly basis, as if somebody had just been smoking and then left. That, and the feeling of a man watching her, was unnerving enough for her that she wanted to keep Brad out of the whole affair. Unlike some of my clients' partners, however, Brad felt something too. It wasn't as intense for him, but he had stayed overnight in the apartment, and experienced the smell and the eerie feeling of being watched to some degree, so he was more than sympathetic to Emily's plight, and keen on having it refreshed for them when he moved in.

I asked Emily to talk to her neighbors and apparently, chain smoking was the habit of the very depressive and somewhat unpleasant man who had lived there prior to her. He had left an energetic stain of the highest order, a combination of anger and depression, detachment, perhaps alcoholism, and constant cigarette smoking while watching TV. That had permanently flavored the apartment, both in a depressive tomb-like sense, and the very noticeable smell of cigarettes, which would mysteriously arrive at night and be gone during the day. The smoking man conducted his meager life during the night, and he was quite interested in observing whoever was living in *his* domain.

Looking through the apartment, I definitely had the uneasy feeling that I was not alone, so I went to work on watching whatever was watching me. What really interested me was that Emily woke up at 3:13 each morning. I was studying Chinese Medicine at the time, and 3 A.M. is the time the lung meridian is activated, cleansing and restoring the lungs in preparation for a new day. For a serious smoker, this could certainly be a time of physical distress, and awakening, so I sat in the chair in the living room (where I suspected he had spent his years alone, watching television) and began to sense.

There was a deep, brooding, anger and detachment there; a feeling of having been counted out of life, and apathy at making any effort to work a way back in. It made me feel sad, for this man, who was not only so trapped in life, but unable to make the transition into death, preferring to memorialize himself in his pain. Repeating his endless cycle of awakening at 3 A.M., he would rise from a passed out stupor in his TV chair to find the screen no longer buzzing with static, miserably wander off to bed, and there he would find himself displaced, by Emily, the living tenant who had overtaken "his" apartment, and angrily, deviously, he would observe her.

Dissolving the energy connections of this man to the apartment, washing the repetitive staining of his burrowing existence out of the walls, clearing his death pictures, escorting him out of this dimension, and erasing the astral plane connection through which he appeared to be watching Emily, was a more intense job than most house clearings I've done. But, while I tell my clients that I rate my service partly on the size of the building, the intensity and duration of the problem is a major factor, and the smoking man had dug himself in. I was happy to have helped Emily and Brad, who I could actually talk to about it, but even more so to release this man whom we would never know.

An interesting note: I rarely make it part of my work to hang out with my clients (although I frequently enjoy them quite a bit), but Emily and Brad and I had such a nice chat that we decided to go out and have dinner before they took me back to the airport. Hanging out and talking with them so much during the closing period of the job, and afterward, I had neglected to fully clean up after myself. So when I called Emily a few days later to check in, she told me that while the place felt really great, that the guy was gone, and the cigarette smoke was gone, she felt like ***I*** was still there. I realized that after having impressed my own energy upon the place so intensely, I had forgotten to remove myself when I left! I quickly sat down to the task, and after that they had a splendid nuptial apartment.

Olfactory Science

Luca Turin, the celebrated olfactory biochemist known as the "Emperor of Smell" has proposed that our smell reception is not mediated (as is commonly accepted) by a molecule's shape, as is the case in other receptors. He asserts that the vibrational speed of the molecule is what defines its odor, and has plenty of evidence to prove it. If this is the case, the Smoking Man, as other smell specific spirits, being remnants of vibratory energy, would clearly carry their smell with them.

Animal Tracks

In animistic cultures, the spirits of the animals bestow different powers and communicate certain information, and the animals themselves are seen as the bearers of those messages. Once in a while, I'm asked to listen to those messages and respond to them. While a casual observer might try to explain freak or oddly directed animal behavior as an outgrowth of habitat issues, when delving into the interconnective web in which we live, I find that animals are informed sources.

Blue Jay Way

Marie Shell called me because her house had a very bizarre problem, being attacked by birds. Although it was the second bird house that I had come across (so I thought it would be a snap), no one ever imagines living with birds that fly smack into the windows and peck at them constantly; and it was wearing on her. An entire flock of blue jays that nested in Marie's backyard would attack the various windows (which forced her to keep them closed all the time), and wake her up by hitting the bedroom early in the morning. Marie also felt uneasy in the backyard and around the house. There was a certain sense of nervousness, anxiety, and sadness, and being referred to me by our mutual friend, she hoped that I could help her out.

When I went over the history of the house with her, my expectations of *another bird job* were quickly dispelled, as this had a character all its own. The original owner, "M", had designed and built the house in the 1930s, and performed all the upkeep and repair himself. In keeping with the idea of keeping an eye on his investments, he built a matching house across the street on the other corner property. One day, while M was working on the roof of the house across the street, he slipped and fell 20 feet to the pavement below, fractured his skull, and died. This happened directly in front of the living room picture window of his home, and was probably seen by one or more of his children. Being so intimately connected to the house as to have designed, built and maintained it in its entirety, his death set a perilous tone for the house contract. The fact that his death was on account of the house's twin also made for a negatively charged, bound energy dynamic between them.

As a result, the landlords who had purchased the house and rented it since then seemed completely unable to handle any of the upkeep. Basic projects had gone undone for years, the building was unkempt and the property was overgrown, and as far as the tenants were concerned, there was no real reason for this. In reviewing the contract with the house it was clear to me that M had contracted *himself* to take care of *everything*. Every kind of project was his duty, and dying so intensely in the face of the house had made it impossible for anyone else to step in and take over. The mere thought of doing maintenance brought with it a gut feeling of the very real possibility of death!

M's accident left his entire family in shock and depression for years afterward as well. Living their lives with the memory of his violent death reflected in each glance out of their picture window created an unconscious desire that there was no house across the street, no house of their own, and most of all, no window to look through. Soon enough, each window became charged with a sense of death lurking outside. This set a somber tone that made it a very difficult place for others to live afterward. Marie had gone through a number of roommates while living there, all of whom had become depressed and had to move. Fortunately for the house, she was somewhat indefatigable, and fortunately for her, she called me.

While the birds were the identified problem, my primary job was to dissolve the deep heart wounding that overwhelmed that house and everyone in it, the energetic connection to and the impact of M's death. It was as if the house hadn't breathed in all those years; and at the risk of a host of blue jays flying though, it really hadn't. The release of M's spirit, and his obligation to repair the house, made a tremendous shift. Separating the energy of the twin houses was also important. They held a mirrored sadness that I wished I could have asked the neighbors if they felt.

Clearing that, and some of the remnant energy of those who had successively lived in the depressed gloom of the house, made things much easier to work with, but there was still the issue of the family, and how their fear had transformed all the windows into points of attack. I went through the house, discharging the stagnant energy patterns in the windows, releasing the memories and bringing them into a present time grounded state. I implemented a new grounding and structural protection for the whole house, which I needed to begin clearing the yard and all of the windows, which I energetically rebuilt to reflect energy outward, rather than feel caved in.

Still, there were the blue jays. I got the feeling that they thought the house was dead, and that they should be able to roost in it, like an old tree. I chatted them up about the fact that this was not the case, and (having eliminated their allowance to act as harbingers of doom from the contract) convinced them that they should abandon their efforts to break in and enjoy the overgrown yard while they could. As a last piece, I spent some time sitting in the back yard, converting it from a threateningly overgrown thicket to a private garden spot.

Quite oddly, just after I was done with the job, and talking to Marie in the kitchen, a blue jay slammed right into the window. It kind of freaked me out, and made me wonder if I had really done *anything*, but I decided to take it as a sign of completion. Sometimes things like that happen, which really make me wonder about this work. I guess I was right, though, as Marie called some weeks later and told me that after I left, the bird attacks stopped completely.

Oh Rats!

Taryn and Roger were clients of my friend Dia, who told them they *needed* to call me. They had purchased a four bedroom house on a creekside in a relatively affluent suburb, but things were not working as they had planned. For starters, Roger was beginning a new business venture, but found that his home office was impossible to organize or work in at anywhere near the level of productivity that he demanded of himself. Here's what he wrote to me.

"The house is constantly in disorder. Things disappear or are misplaced. It feels oppressive and depressive sometimes. There is hopelessness in living here. Things break all the time, and odd things happen. The garage door fell off. It literally "Popped its bolts." I asked the door guy, 'Is this normal?' 'No, it's not.' he replied. Workmen have had accidents working on the house, and we have had to replace more than the normal amount. Taryn says 'You can be in a good mood until you come into the house, then you become angry.' The children have mixed feelings about the house too."

The greatest physical manifestation of difficulty with the house, however, was the rat problem. In fact, when they first called me, they asked me if I could do something about rats. They had an inconceivable rat problem. The city had come out and been unable to do anything. The top rat specialist in the region had been there repeatedly, trapped the biggest rat of his career, and refused to charge them because he couldn't get the job done.

I'd never been asked to deal with rats before, and when they described the problem I felt it would be quite overreaching of me to say that I *could* get rid of them. But, while I know what I *can do,* I never ***really*** know what I *can't.* I had asked a colony of black widow spiders to move that year, and they did, so, recognizing that there were probably more things going on than the worst rat infestation I had ever heard of, I agreed to take the job and see.

The clue that there was more going than rats had to do with Roger and Taryn's *awareness* of this house, and its sort of caved-in feeling. They told me that they had toured 150 houses, which is quite a few, looking for the right one. While they were at it, they had driven by this one and ignored its For Sale sign at least three times before ever stopping to check it out. It certainly wasn't in a bad neighborhood, or visibly in physical disrepair, but I'm sure it didn't feel too good, because in all that time no one else bought it either. Finally, the desperation of searching for a house set in, and when they stumbled onto it again they decided that they could refurbish it to the standard they wanted to live in. Unfortunately, the house itself had some other ideas.

The woman who sold them the house, Mrs. G, had owned it since it was built, in the mid-sixties. She and her husband had a son, Ricky, who had been diagnosed as schizophrenic while in his teens. In his early 20s, Ricky committed suicide, perhaps after moving out on his own. Taryn wasn't sure if this was before or after his father's death, which also occurred around that time, but events seemed to be linked energetically. I don't think Ricky killed himself there at the house, but it appeared to me that his spirit definitely returned there.

Years later, Mrs. G married a man who then moved into the house with her. Over time, he wound up developing macular degeneration, and was rapidly approaching blindness. This forced them to sell the house and move somewhere that could accommodate them better, a fact which Taryn and Roger told me he seemed very bitter about.

The neighboring house was owned by Don, a doctor who had moved there with his young family in 1974. He and Ricky became good friends before Ricky's death, and perhaps something about the suicide spurred him on to become a psychiatrist. He was now relegated to his house, however, due to brain lesions that had left him unable to lead his professional life or really care for himself. As a result of this, his back yard had become completely overgrown, a veritable jungle of trees and vines, which the rats colonized and made into their hidden fortress.

The house had a big sunken living room which was adjacent to Don's house. There was an overgrown fence between them, on which I could see rats climbing and descending in a constant stream while I was working there. This living room, while wonderfully appointed, was mostly left unused, probably because it maintained the feeling of being Ricky's hangout. It also adjoined the kitchen, which was the scene of numerous mishaps, breakdowns of every appliance and lighting fixture, and workmen's accidents; innumerable problems that the house seemed to present as Taryn and Roger attempted to remodel it.

Clearly, I had work to do, but still, I felt something else going on, and had to ask Taryn *where* the rats actually infiltrated the house. Strangely enough, they would climb over the fence, go all the way around to the other side of the house, and head up into the roof beams, where they were eating their way into the attic above the master bedroom. In examining *that* room, I was met with such a tremendous sense of grief that the room itself felt as if it were caving in on itself.

Suffering the loss of her husband and the tragic death of their son was a heart crushing combination, and on top of it, Mrs. G was wracked with guilt; manifested by the rats gnawing away at her physical domain. In marrying her second husband, she really tried to resume living, but still bore the brunt of her tragedy. I doubt she was ever able to fully recover, and as she withdrew into her sadness the rats chewed into the roof above her bedroom, so that her nights were alive with the scratching menace - as perhaps was her own mind.

Her second husband, as he descended into blindness, was livid over having to leave the house, even though his situation demanded it. In classic irony, it turned out that *his* den was the room that Roger had chosen for an office. This sort of made me snicker, as I find a certain humor in the way in which these energetic patterns play out, and the results they create in my clients' lives. This room was painted with the sense of what it would be to be going blind: to be decreasingly capable of seeing, the panicked emotional resonance and how it physically altered life. This was the embedded sense of this room, in which my client Roger was attempting to start an extremely *visionary* business, a radical new technology with a completely new networking system! Roger certainly had the capacity, connections, and capability to do this, but he couldn't find his own business cards on top of his desk! It was impossible for him to sort out his work area, let alone do extremely visionary design work, *because the room in which he was trying to do it was so deeply flavored by the feeling of encroaching blindness that there was no way for him to see!*

Those were the primary emotional investments that I was called upon to remove, release, and reset, and it was not an easy task. Dealing with the embedded manifestations of Ricky's suicide came first, and in suicide situations the misdirected energy of spirit commonly results in poltergeist phenomena. Electrical difficulties, breakdowns of machinery and appliances, these things come with the territory. It seemed that Ricky's territory went from hanging out on the couch, to the refrigerator, and perhaps the garage, the exact corridor of electrical failure and workmen's mishaps.

A thorough cleansing of the electrical and mechanical systems was required to disconnect his energy from the house, and that had me crawling through the wiring and into every appliance. Still, there was the residual energy of his spirit, his emotional connection to both his mother *and to Don,* pulling the rats across the fence as if he were commanding an army to shout "*I'm here! I'm here!*" Forgiving his spirit and releasing him from the need to be seen made a tremendous shift.

Working with the self-enfolding grief of Mrs. G *(which Taryn validated for me in discussing her own sense that her bedroom felt inwardly collapsing),* was another primary piece of work. Filling her imploded heart with and endless stream of the roses that still grew outside, washing her in forgiveness and sending her energy down the creek to return to her, was key to restoring the energy structure of the whole house, before it caved in, Usher like, on itself. Discharging the bristling anger of (and restoring the light that was being lost to) the second husband was essential to restoring Roger's ability to work.

Returning to the rat problem, and their colony next door, it was abundantly clear that separations from Don and his house needed to be made. Ricky's death had a great impact on Don, and greatly influenced the way he approached his own children. Perhaps their energetic connection had some influence on the brain condition he suffered, it's impossible to say, but I made what separations I could between them, then layered walls of energy around and between both properties. Of course I did a thorough cleansing, grounding and resetting of the house, as well as some minor touch up for the kids, before I watched what appeared to be the last rat departing over the fence. When I spoke to Taryn a week later, it turned out that what I went into the job unable to guarantee *(or even really expect much possibility of),* was resolved. Not only did the house feel completely new, inviting and supportive, the plague of rats had completely left the premises.

In The Office

While the majority of my work has been in homes, our workplaces also seethe with interpersonal dynamics, and occasionally accidents, deaths or disasters that would call for energy work. A common theme in Feng Shui is — never open a restaurant (or any business) where the prior has gone out of business. I see it all the time, the held energy of a failed business making it impossible for a new one to take hold. In that light, most of my business clients have been quite progressive, choosing to enlist my aid on the front end, before everything hits the fan.

Management Shakeup

Erin B was a student at *the Academy*, working in the art department of an ad agency in San Francisco. They were very hip, did a lot of early Internet advertising and electronic media stuff, but had recently undergone a management change. The director who had departed was described by Erin as "a real bitch." She was disliked by the entire staff, mostly for the fact that she was excessively controlling, selfish, and acted as if she were 'above it all'. Her employees felt that they were under her surveillance, and this created a feeling of resentment which in turn lowered productivity.

After she left, the new manager, Mark, spoke to Erin about how unpleasant it felt to sit in the office of his predecessor. Erin gave him her honest appraisal of the cumulative anger directed toward it, which had been increasing over the last year. Personally, Erin liked *Mark* very much, but there was a generalized sense of anger and suspicion directed toward the physical space he had taken over, and the staff looked toward his door with a sense of distrust and worry. This completely confirmed his own sense of how things felt there.

Mark had traveled the world extensively, and was very spiritual. He *sensed* that some kind of space cleansing was needed and asked Erin if she knew of any shaman types who did that kind of thing. When she called to ask me about the job I was thrilled, because it was a completely new challenge, so without her even telling Mark, she brought me in to clear their office; on a Saturday, of course.

I had worked on a number of small business spaces by then, several therapy offices, some restaurants, but nothing like this. Their office was in a major highrise, on the 21st floor! It was a beautiful building, lots of glass, great views, but it struck me primarily with a heretofore unimagined objective - How to ground an office, or a particular floor, within a building of thirty floors? More specifically, how to ground a building from twenty floors up?

Obviously, I wasn't being hired to do the whole building *(although I'd gladly take the job),* so I had to determine just how to go about grounding this structure quickly and effectively. Having done some personal grounding work at altitude (in planes for instance) it was not completely beyond me conceptually. In my own body, I know what I need to do to connect to earth energy, however weak the signal, but the objective here was to pull a column of earth energy from deep underground to the upper floors of the building.

Usually, when working in an apartment, say, I'm close enough to the ground to get a feel of the earth, and I can pull it though the structure, or use a specific technique to quickly ground all the matter in between. Here I was floating, and didn't want to pull through two million cubic feet of building space. So I expanded myself throughout the entire floor, until I was wall to wall, and rode the superstructure of the building down into the earth, energetically connecting there and pulling a current of earth energy back up through the framework, which I spread across that entire floor of the building. (*It was a stunning bit of work, if I do say so myself.*)

The feeling throughout the office, however, of being watched, spied on, and suspected, was definitely a stain that would still be difficult for people to work around, so I spent a couple of hours moving throughout the different cubicles, dissolving and returning the web of inquisitorial energy to the fired manager, and to what had been her office, my final destination. My intention was to sit in that office and re-vision the way that it worked; to alter the objective of management so it could operate in a multilateral radial, rather than a pyramidal fashion.

I concentrated on wiping the imprint of the previous manager and her entire management style, and imbuing the space with the feeling of a supported, interconnecting network centering around Mark. I imbedded a new contract stating that this was an open-door office and that one's position as employee was to be connected and responsible for one's own work. It turned out that Mark was much more interested in working with everyone on the team to assess and optimize their responsibility levels than to try and micromanage and oversee what they did. Sitting in his executive chair in his window-facing-the-Bay office, I was able to really cement the "man in the tower's" astute, well-rounded, yet connected feeling; exactly what was called for.

Sinking myself down through the outer beams of the building, through its foundation, and further down into the earth hundreds of feet below me, I reset my column of earth energy, giving all the changes a solid grounding to work from. It was a very positive change for their office, and my friend Erin not only reported a significant increase in workplace productivity and morale, but told me that Mark recognized the change immediately that following Monday, without anything being said.

Live Work

IN OUR MODERN WORLD, IT's hard to remember that until the age of the factory, people almost always worked out of their homes. They lived upstairs, or out back, but perhaps they defined themselves more by their work, and didn't realize that they had a life to be living as well. What I see in many Live Work situations is that people fail to separate their lives, allowing their business affairs to overrun their homes and setting the tone of their energy and their emotional response patterns to an inappropriate mode for family life.

Back at the Ranch

Dana was a graduate of *the Academy* whose ranch had been her home for over forty years. She had grown up there with her adoptive parents, survived their deaths, been married, divorced, and remarried (and almost completed the attendant child rearing) without ever moving. After her *Academy* training, she realized that she needed to change the decades-old, constricting energy patterns of her house, as well tune up the property and her relationship to it.

Dana's parents had both been alcoholics, and her second marriage had recently fallen to alcoholism as well. Fortunately, she was not the drinker, but she saw this codependent life pattern needing to be broken before her children, who were verging on adulthood, fell down the well. As the property was a working ranch, with kennels and horse corrals and land use projects, she was quite busy overseeing its business aspects, and had very little time off. There was something of an open door between the business ends of the ranch and her home, which was in the center of the property. Without much differentiation between her personal space and the workspace, her moments of home life were constantly being intruded upon. That and the fact that her home itself was filled with energetic ties to the past (including the presence of her dead parents), made it a very restless place to live.

The ranch was a beautiful property, which I spent some time walking in order to connect to the local earth energy. I knew I'd need it to ground the house, which was a very interesting structure as well. The central beam of the living room was a ship's mast, and its wood paneling was salvaged as well from a schooner that wrecked on the beach nearby a century before. Perhaps its age-old sense of grog-drenched tragedy set the tone to begin with. Her parents had spent a great deal of time in that dark old living room, sitting in their drinking chairs, instilling the alcoholic behavior patterning that Dana had grown up in.

The energy that they had left with their own deaths made the living room in particular feel *(if not that they were* still there *drinking*), that one should be sitting by the fire drinking. It was the template for living; the behavioral groove that had been cut into that room. That was not a groove of behavior that Dana wanted to live with anymore, particularly as she was facing her second son's first strike at independence, and already knew what that might mean.

The remnants of stuck energy in her bedroom from the drunken battles with her ex-spouses, combined with that — *just have a drink* — feel, made it a difficult space for her to feel at home with anymore. It was powerful work for me, to open this darkened wood, firelit remoteness to the tremendous open sky and forest around them. Releasing what energy of her parents remained, and dissolving their contract for a life colored by bottle glass, began the process, during which I experienced some of the tragic moments of Dana's upbringing and relationship demise. Creating the sense of home and safety for Dana and her children also required disconnecting her exes' energy from the house, giving her a sense of finally *ending* those relationships, and some dissolution of their own alcohol tinged family patterning.

It was a multi-leveled job, with various externals to deal with around the business issues. After a discussion of the necessity of separating her personal and business lives on an energetic level, I had to work with the other players in the ranch businesses, set up an "energetic organizational chart," so to speak, so that each had a defined energetic space and controlled level of interaction with Dana. This resulted in a major resetting of their (near nonexistent) boundaries, both in a human sense and with the physical structures that comprised the ranch. It was clear that Dana needed to close the door to the business world to live in her home world, and that would require new rules and boundaries regarding the office space and her relation to it.

She stayed in the house throughout the tuning, and said that it was quite an emotional experience for her. She felt the lifting the veils of her past and the pain lodged within various chapters, from her parents and spouses, but it created a much better environment for her and her family, and increased prosperity for the ranch. Not long after I worked there, Dana met a very stable gentleman whom she began dating. That evolved into his working on the ranch, then helping to run it, and eventually, a happy marriage for both of them.

Net-Worked

The Hartfords bought a 60's tract house in Marin, knowing that it had some history of high turnover as a rental. It had been a bit of a rowdy and unsettled place for a number of years before the owners prior to them, who after a difficult few years of their own, decided to sell. Kurt and Jean had been through their own struggles since moving in, both with taking custody of Kurt's daughters and growing them out to independence, and forming their own business, which had since consumed the house. Kurt was a network engineer who built an ISP, complete with rooms full of servers and routers right there in their house. That took up much of his attention, and Jean's as well, and seemed to be diverting them from their home life.

Many of my clients work from their home offices, as do I, and I'd venture to say that most of them find their lives bleeding into each other. It's important to create a level of separation between home and business, but with the more invasive or inescapable technologies of wireless systems and routing of electronics throughout a house, it's becoming more and more difficult to maintain that separation, and having all those electronic brains around demands more and more attention paid to them.

The reason that the Hartfords called me was a lack of focus about the house and an inability to get work done, on any level. Jean found herself unable to meditate or do her personal work, and Kurt too found his computer projects bogging down as everything spun slowly in an entropic storm. From the outset it appeared that the long-term residue and discord of 20 years of renters, whose demands for repairs went ignored by the original owner, set the contract of the house in antipathy toward anything being completed, and that contract held. Kurt and Jean found themselves stymied. Even though it needed work, the house itself seemed to refuse their efforts to improve it, and that was getting to be a bit disheartening. This sense of struggle extended into their relationship and to their relationship with Kurt's daughters as well. All of this left them feeling somewhat drained and besieged by the idea of moving ahead with anything.

As a rental, the house had always been more of a way station than a home in which someone really set their intention for living, and that jumble left quite a bit of energetic debris to be cleared. The Hartfords had a pretty clear intention of what they wanted, but in rewriting the contract for them to really inhabit the place, I found that the dual nature of their house as a thriving computer hub and a family home were somewhat in competition, and I needed to make special arrangements to suit this. I not only *emptied the cache,* deleting the house's history of frustration and breakdown, I reprogrammed all of the things that they needed to structurally support their business, and their lives as well.

They needed to be able to step out of the office and into their living room, or out to the poolside, and to interface *as humans,* appreciate the natural area of Marin in which they lived, play with their animals (and each other), and breathe outside the electromagnetic pulsation that emanated from their office and snaked its way in CAT-10 cable through their house. I find that it's fairly difficult to work in a computer environment and maintain one's standard autonomic nervous settings, but a ghost hunter's equipment would have gone wild from the amount of EMF radiation there.

This overdrive may be causing a lot of illness in our computer-driven culture. There's been some research to support this conclusion, and few ideas about how to *deal* with it. The Hartford home was completely infiltrated by the Borg of their computer work, and that was definitely affecting them. The main office was networked through their bedroom into other rooms until the octopus-like configuration of computer energy reached almost every part of the house. This required me to install a special kind of shielding, from as much of the EMF as one can hope for (working strictly on a psychic energy level), and from the energy body considerations that come into play with neurological alignment to computer clock speeds, information throughput, and the like.

It was important to enclose the workspace, to energetically firewall their separate computer projects from each other's, and shield the entirety from the rest of the house. I used computer models where I could, overlaying a circuit board imprint of the house's sectors and installing switches and gates that stepped them into different modes when moving through one life door to another, with the sort of energetic shielding that allowed Kurt and Jean to work both separately and cooperatively, and to live their lives fully within the same atmospheric continuum that held their business.

Positive outcomes always seem to accrue from appropriately applied intention, and both of them acknowledged, over the ensuing months, that business and the house were looking better than ever. Their increased functionality at work, in their relationship, and on an internally focused level, all grew out of their intentionally rehabilitated space. My work there was quite eye opening for me too, leading me to develop a class on maintaining one's energy field when working around computers, and specific practices that are quite valuable for me as a writer and web developer.

Death Itself

WHILE MY WORK TAKES ME all over the energetic map, death is *my department*. We all have to die some day, and rarely get to choose the why, when and where. Those of us who aren't totally panicked about death itself are panicked about simply trying to die with some dignity. It's brought me a great sense of compassion; sorting through people's fear, loss, longing, grief and tragedy, and trying to resolve whatever binds their spirit to this world, when they clearly no longer belong. The question of how they leave an imprint, or how their spirit manifests in the material world, will always be a question. But it's clear to me that intention, whether willful or misguided, is a driving force.

Coming Home

One hits turning points in life, moments that instill real belief, or disbelief. It's probably rare that work leads people to these moments, but my work has always bordered on unbelievable, so the line wasn't far off. After a few years I had grouted together a certain irrational acceptance of what I did, my clients' need for it, and the changes that it affected, but I still found myself fighting my own skepticism. Like my clients, I was never prepared to be convinced.

Denise Darling called me after being referred to me, quite oddly, from two or three different people. It's pretty rare that anyone's rolodex would include that many people who even know I exist, but she was edging up against my circle. Within a period of a few months she had gone from a fairly well-centered psychotherapist to fearing that she was going insane, and had begun suffering from inexplicable leg pains as well, so she *needed* to find me. She had moved into a flat, the lower unit of a two-story house in Oakland, right down the street from Lake Merritt.

When she first looked at the house, with the rental agent, it was apparent that the prior tenant had left in a hurry. Most of their belonging were still there, unpacked. There were still dirty dished in the sink, and stuff out on the counter, as if somebody had just packed a bag and split. The property manager had actually been dating the tenant, and he had agreed to pack all of her stuff and send it out to her, after she had "decided to move back east to live with her mother."

Denise found that to be rather strange, but for a rational person it didn't seem like a terribly overwhelming ordeal to ignore it and move in. Not long after she and her roommate Ann had unpacked, however, they began to feel strange; unsettled, apprehensive, unhealthy, but nothing "real". The first undeniable sign that something was wrong came a month later when their cat began to get sick. Lucy was not an old cat, she had always been healthy, but she began to simply degenerate before their eyes. The vets didn't have a clue as to what was wrong, but Lucy was getting sicker every day, just curling up and dying.

Denise became very concerned, not only for the fact that her cat was probably going to die, but for the fact that she felt a presence there, a sadness, and an implacable, indefinable disease with living there. There were also some phenomenological problems, lights turning on and off, phone ringing with no one there, things like that. It began to really get under her skin, and she became worried that she was losing her sanity, even though Ann was suffering from similar feelings, albeit (for reasons which will become clear) not as intensely.

One of Denise's friends worked with a psychic, who referred her to me, but that sounded too weird, so she didn't call. Another friend showed her my ad, but she didn't call. She and Ann did ask one of their intuitive friends to come over and look at the house, but that woman got violently ill and was knocked out for about three days after trying to work there. Finally Denise was referred to me by the manager of The Floatation Center, a place where we both rented time in isolation tanks. That gave her a trusted point of reference, so she finally called me. It was quite interesting, discussing all of these phenomena and her concern over losing her rational mind from them, and whether hiring me was actually the final step toward being insane. Eventually I convinced her (although she didn't take too much convincing) to have me work on the house.

I wanted to get as much background on the house as I could, so we spoke to her neighbor, who had known the woman who owned the house. The neighbor told us that the old woman lived with her husband, who had died some years prior, but always alone, they had no children, never spoke of any, and just lived in the upstairs of the house. Quite oddly, it seemed to me, as the houses on that street had been single-family dwellings, and this had been converted many years prior to upper and lower flats by the old woman and her husband. They had walled off the staircase, and completely separated the units.

That didn't seem odd in the sense of rental property in the Bay Area. It's quite financially attractive to have a home large enough to divide if you want to retire to the upstairs of the house. The odd part of it was that this lower unit of the house had gone vacant for twenty years. They hadn't retired on rental income, they just walled off the downstairs and left it empty. Only after her husband died did the old woman start to rent it. Of course, no one stopped to consider this. To think something was odd about that, you'd have to think odd things.

As I began to feel my way around the house and sense the very palpable discomfort and dis-ease, it became a big question for me. I too like to put a story to the sense of what I'm feeling, and the idea that this was just another house didn't fit the feeling at all. Death and grief overwhelmed me as I sifted through the layers of energy there, and I had to work harder than ever to maintain my separation and clarity. I worked my way through the house, grounding and clearing what I could from the different rooms, and finally I came to sit in Denise's bedroom. She was working at her desk there, and asked me if she could stay and watch. "Sure, if you'd like," I told her.

For the past month, mind you, Denise had been suffering from completely inexplicable leg pains. They had started hampering her ability to walk, and this was really beginning to freak her out. She was now not only mentally on edge, but was physically in a very strange predicament — all since moving into this house, and (from my perspective) from *living* in this house. I sat down on her bed and focused my attention on the feeling that surrounded us. It felt like death, grief, and an incredible yearning to be home. I could sense a thread, as if this energy had pulled itself into the room from another location, by force of will.

I plugged myself into the energy trail, and instantly was somewhere else, *some*one else. I was in the jungle, in Vietnam, a young soldier on patrol, nervously hiking through a small clearing, clutching an M-16, alert, keyed up, stepping.... *on a landmine!* Flash blinded, deafened, and thrown into the air, the searing pain was only momentary, but the shock of landing and starting to run, only to find that my legs weren't attached to the stumps twitching below me, threw me into a screaming panic. As a firefight engulfed the friends who couldn't help me, I lay there dying, my young life, with all my dreams, all my plans, and all my love for my parents, slipping away. Shot from my body like the blast that had dismembered me, my spirit flew back to the comfort and safety of my room, still as I had left it after high school. My Mother, *My Mother! My Father! I must tell them that I love them!* I can't leave this way, in this jungle, to rot. *I have to go home!*

In that moment I saw that this was the son of the people who had owned and divided the house. This was the son who had never been spoken of to the neighbors, because the grief was so great, and more so because his energetic presence in the house, constantly trying to connect to them, was so intense that they sealed off the downstairs and left it locked for 20 years.

This "energetic event picture" required a lot of clearing, both to dissolve the still bristling intercontinental column of energy, and to enable me to sit with the remnant spirit of this boy, nineteen, perhaps twenty, dying so terribly, summoning all of his being to return home, to his family, and finding no means of connecting to them because he was now dead. The intensity of pain of his dismemberment, the loss of his young life and his connection to his family, poisoned this room, and made it a crippling nightmare of a place to be. All of his spirit energy was trapped there, seeking connection, redemption, forgiveness that had never come, because the phenomenon of his return was too terrifying to deal with.

Thankful to be wearing my mullah (a Tibetan Buddhist prayer necklace), I went to work on reviewing and releasing the energy of his death, clearing his spirit from this dimension, from his connection to Vietnam, from this room, from his attempted reconnection to his mother and father, and from the house in general. When I was done, the feeling of having sucked this blackness out of the room and out of the house was like the proverbial white tornado, *which in fact was what I visualized to do it.* When I was done, I opened my eyes and Denise, who had been sitting at her desk this whole time, was staring at me, jaw agape. "What did you just do?!" she asked me. Even as a complete naïf to this type of work, she had felt the polar shift in the energy of the room, and within her own body, which was apparently becoming debilitated by energetic proximity to the young man's loss of limb.

I tried to explain in some sort of layman's term the level of the work I was doing, how I had just sort of transited the boy's spirit from this dimension, but it was more than a little awkward, so I went to work on completing the rest of my task and went home. When I checked in with Denise a week later to see what was going on, she was really astounded. Not only did she feel normal, sane, and happy, Ann felt the same way. What's more, her leg pain had completely disappeared, and her Lucy had inexplicably begun a complete recovery.

She also told me that she called her property manager, and asked him if she could contact his ex-girlfriend, to ask about her experience there. He told her that he knew the house was haunted, and it had been a problem, and that he was sorry he didn't tell her. She called his ex, the former tenant, who told her, " I couldn't handle it there anymore, the feel of the place, things moving around at night. I was hearing this voice speaking to me, the sounds were making me so frightened that one night I just packed some clothes in a duffel bag and drove back to Michigan."

That job, more than any other, clarified for me the intensity of the energy question and the veracity of my work.

Malevolent Presence

On rare occasion, I'm invited to work in a house that holds the energy of someone who died with so much negativity that they have no interest in healing, forgiveness, resolution, or anything but maintaining their spiteful, angry presence on this plane. Even when I can see into their injury, and find compassion for them, their hate is far too well established, and the effect they have on their homes makes my clients extremely happy to find me.

Curses!

Denise Kelly had heard about my work and considered for a very long time whether or not to call me. She had actually gotten my name from some students at the Academy and called me a year prior, in an attempt to refer me to one of her friends whose property had a "serious" problem. She felt she was dealing pretty well with her own situation, so it didn't occur to her to use me herself, despite the fact that she and her husband both heard voices, and the occasional cries of a baby, although her nearest neighbors were a mile away. Denise reported to me a number of anomalies about the place, things constantly going missing and reappearing, odd sounds, voices, but that was the least of it.

In the room that she had originally set up as her daughter's bedroom, her daughter, who was quite young, maybe three at that time, had terrible nightmares. She would wake up crying and get in their bed every night, and they found that was just too much to deal with, so Denise converted it into a day-room cum office with a little guest/nap-bed, which she often used, although it always made her somehow uncomfortable, as it did most of her guests.

Over time, she found that when she would nap there in the afternoon, she would often feel that a man had lain down next to her, depressing the mattress and pulling at the covers, and that she would feel his cold presence next to her. Or, as it happened, when she would awake at night and be unable to go back to sleep, and try to sleep on the little bed, that she would be haunted by very difficult dreams, dreams of an elderly man, who was tormenting her.

The day before she called to hire me, she had a dream in which the man was grabbing her and she was paralyzed. He was squeezing her hand, and dragging her along against her will. When she woke up from this dream, she had marks on her hand, as if she had been clawed by fingernails. This was obviously more than she had bargained for, or wanted to have in her home, so she decided that it was time to have me come and clean up the situation.

To begin with, her home had an incredible history. It was over a century old, built out from the one-room farmhouse of the original property owners of that valley, who farmed a pretty large section. Their daughter Lillian had become involved with a man, Bob Gaines, and married him. Around the time that they became married her parents died, and in the embittered division of the property (between eight grown children), she was given the house, along with a miniscule corner of their land on which to move it. When I looked at the situation, what I intuited was that her family was not at all happy with her choice of suitors, and that Bob may have been thinking that he was marrying his way into vast property holdings. Being given the house with no property and no option to farm, Bob was very upset and made Lillian's life very difficult, constantly ordering her around, demeaning and physically abusing her, as it appeared he continued doing in Denise's dreams.

Denise had also heard that the Lillian suffered a stillborn child, and I felt that this may have led to Bob Gaines to cursing her, her family, and the property. There was a feeling that I registered of a very long held and deeply embedded curse energy, as if the whole property had been damned by this man, who was obviously very angry, and seemed a rather scurrilous, scamming bastard, if you will. That curse energy left an incredible imprint. He drove his young wife (the rightful owner of the valley) through an unhappy life to an untimely death, and carried on his dissolute existence there until he died, always with a sense of anger and indignation.

The property probably changed hands a few times before being purchased by a man named Ron Middleton. He was a local contractor who became notorious for murdering one of his subcontractors, a carpet installer, rolling him up in a carpet, and dumping him in the creek bed behind the house. He dumped some construction trash over it and hired a caterpillar to fill in that section, which was dry at that time of year. That's how he ended up being reported, arrested, and convicted for the murder.

Whether he killed his worker in the house or elsewhere is uncertain, but the incident certainly left a weird vibe, and made the house something of a stagnant property as far as real estate is concerned. However, another family purchased it, and refurbished a lot of it, before leaving rather abruptly. For people investing in property, and certainly for the amount of work that they had put into it, I'm sure that a number of things made them feel uncomfortable, because they definitely took a loss in a boom market.

When I looked into the layering around Ron Middleton (who's still in prison for murder), it seemed that Bob Gaines had been making an impact on him, colluding with him in his own psychic detachment. Apparently Mr. Middleton had been a heavy drinker and cocaine user, and I got the impression of his spending a lot of time in the house inebriated, perhaps unable to sleep without dreaming of Bob Gaines and his ill intent. Mr. Middleton began to lose his way, and whether the argument that he had with his carpeting contractor was over some drugs or his lack of payment for work done, it was never quite established. However, the influence of the house and Bob Gaines definitely added to his decision to kill his friend, and to attempt to bury him there.

Working my way back to the original contracts with Bob Gaines and Lillian's family, I could see that the house was really in a dysfunctional state. Being moved from its original location, while in the midst of a hostile family negotiation, following the death of the original owners and the ill-advised marriage of their daughter, superseded by years of Bob Gaines' hatred and cursing, all made it a lonely, desolate place, perversely tucked away in the midst of a lush farming valley. So, my first piece of work was to connect the property to the very earth-bound setting of the region.

Walking the perimeter, it was very easy to be deeply in contact with the earth energy, but there within the house, it was almost alien. Sitting on the deck I could feel that cursing of the land, pushing life itself away from the house like the spit of a prospector who'd died working on dead claim. The deep sadness of Lillian, who had grown up there, losing her family in the split and her child along the way, left a tremendous sadness as well, which Denise seemed to constellate around from her own life struggle.

Being a century-old, the house began as a one-room affair, with the kitchen and sleeping areas in different corners. The bad bedroom had been walled off about the time the house was moved. Denise and her children lived in additions to the house that had been added by Ron Middleton or the people who bought it from him. The master bedroom and the children's bedroom felt completely different than the main house, having nothing to do with its energy, but the intensity of the way that room felt was grinding.

Occasionally I run into these cases, where the primary negative entity doesn't want to be forgiven, seek release, or resolution, and dissolving their energy and connection at every anchor point requires a lot of specific observation and work on my part. Mr. Gaines was certainly not a happy man, and he reveled in making life unpleasant for whoever entered "his" space. He had no interest in leaving, either. While I felt ethically responsible about eliminating him, he had been so well entrenched on the astral plane that it took quite an effort to track down all of his forms. I was able to clear out his remnant energy, but it took some time, and some specific disconnection from Denise, who had become attached to him.

It was in reclaiming the sacredness of the land, asking it to return in spirit, after having been banished for so long, that oddly made everything look different, as if a filter had been removed and the true color revealed. Reconnecting the house to the land, so that the feeling of this beautiful secluded place could really be connected to and lived with, allowed me to finish the work; dissolving the sadness of Lillian Gaines, whose losses set the cornerstone of grief upon which all her husband's anger rested. When that breath was finally taken, the home became a place that Denise and her family could finally create their happy and connected existence.

There was a little residual teasing out to be done, as a door slammed before I left, and Bob had one last hurrah that night, but I followed up with Denise and made sure to "close all the windows," after which things settled into the pastoral feeling that was meant to be.

Suicide

As I said, we rarely get to choose the why, when and where of our passing, and those who do are usually making the terrible mistake of thinking escaping *this* life means escaping life itself. I spoke to a friend who had attempted suicide once, who told me that it was the most difficult thing he ever did, and that every nerve in his body was magnetically repelling him, screaming, "Don't Jump!" Even in cases where the voices are telling one *to* end it, the battle for self-preservation is strong, and in the aftermath, release is still the highest goal.

Sorry Mom

David Stockton purchased a small, older bungalow in Venice, just before the boom had crept far enough east from the beach to make it too expensive. It was a quaint house in a quiet neighborhood, with an expansive backyard, sort of a wide open jungly area that had been very exquisitely gardened by the woman who had owned it, but now was somewhat in disrepair, a project house. It had a very old one-car garage that had opened onto the alley behind it, and a newer two-part garage that had been built across the yard from that. When David moved in, he found himself very much invested in these two buildings. He turned the smaller garage into a very nice working studio and he found himself gravitating to it, because the house itself felt *uncomfortable*. He cleaned up the two-car garage and made it his storage area, another useful space on the property, but the house itself was of much less use to him.

The kitchen was functional, but the main bedroom, which opened with French doors into the backyard, became more of a transit point. The front bedroom, which he had intended to use as his office, became more of a storage locker. Centering his life in the back yard, he found himself sleeping on the couch in his studio office pretty frequently, or camping out in the yard itself, because he disliked the feel of his house. As time went on, he noticed his discomfort in the house more and more, and one day discussed this with his neighbor. She had been there for 30-40 years, and knew the woman who had owned the house, Martha, who lived there for 50 years, before she was moved off to a rest home and died.

Martha had two sons, and while he was still in high school, her younger son committed suicide. He shot himself, in the front bedroom, and she discovered him there. The feeling of her son's anguish at having left such a terrible stain upon his mother's house, *and upon her very life,* made his inability to ever apologize a burden that weighed on that room ever since. Unable to forgive himself, he was also unable to escape the physical confines of the human plane, and that final memory picture, of his death mess, became an image imbedded in the consciousness of the walls. The grief that his mother carried, in living there for 30 years after this event, was unmistakable. She managed her life, investing most of it in her garden, but the ever-present awareness of her son's remnant energy, and that last brutal vision of him, left her with a smothering grief which she could never escape.

This is what David told me about the house — "Odd feelings in the front room, or within line of site from its doorway. Feeling Not Alone. Cold and the hair on the back of my neck stands up. The room has a cheesy '70s wood paneling that I feel is hiding traces of the event. I feel a man's deep isolation, sadness and despair, and have seen flashes of a body splayed in the corner, blood everywhere. I see this from the doorway, the same place his mother did. I feel her reeling back, devastated, screaming, hysterical, I feel their sadness. I think he can't leave, he did this terrible thing to himself IN HIS MOM'S HOUSE. She is trying to forgive him and I feel that I am an intruder."

That front bedroom, which David had been unable to use, *even as an office*, had become (as I find these rooms often become in my clients' houses) a junk room. A very, very, *expensive* junk room. David's ability to focus, organize, sort out, clean up, arrange, or determine what to do with his stuff, work, or with the room itself, was completely stymied. And whenever he entered that room his feelings shifted, varying between depressed sadness and heart-stricken grief. This, of course, was why he was referred to me.

David was one of the few *men*, who as clients, have been clear about the difficult energy of their home, and who, having it explained to them, really understood it, recognizing how it matched their emotional experience of it. Going through this whole thing clarified to him what *I* see when I come to a house - the obvious anomaly that someone would be living in their garage, and sleeping out in their backyard! Because it was wonderful, sunny old Venice, where you *could* camp out in the backyard most of the year, you might not realize how that decision would point to a *need* to avoid a situation that you were not fully comprehending the impact of.

The studio that David had refurbished was quite comfortable, attractive, and of course, had none of the unpleasant feelings. No one had been living in the ancient garage. The yard and gardens were coming back to life under his hand, and did not hold the tremendous sense of loss that one was punched in the heart with at the moment of crossing the threshold, which intensified when walking into that front room, where David himself could feel the presence of the dead boy and his grief-stricken mother.

Sitting in that room, cloaked in sorrow, there was an obvious need to bring forgiveness to this boy, to lift his decades-old trapped energy up and out of the house, and connect it to the light. He had suffered, enough in life to mistakenly think that he could end it, and from then on as a trapped spirit, with unbearable guilt over the suffering he caused, in his misguided attempt to escape it. I felt for him, delivered all the blessings I could bestow, and with his departure, began the atomic wall washing of the death picture that I could plainly see.

From there I began to lift the grief that surrounded the event, which was reinforced each day as his mother returned to the house to find herself not quite alone. Fortunately, her intensive gardening had created a grounding connection that still held, allowing me to open the house to the secluded nature setting that really existed, to empty the years of loss out the French doors of her room, and bury them. That garden path was quite valuable in resetting how things felt there, so that David was able to bring his life into alignment. Centered still in the garden, but connected to the whole house (*and living in his bedroom*), David could finally make us of his whole property, and turn his studio back into the creative place that it was *intended* to be, rather than the remote corner his house's pain had forced him into.

When I saw David again, a year ago, I couldn't recognize his house. The feel of it was that different. It had become a hideaway, a sanctuary from the intensity that *is* LA. David showed me through, and it all looked great. He had redone the front room, and told me that beneath the paneling he had found blood splattered and bone fragments in the walls. From the looks of it now, you would never know, or even have an inkling, the energy was so different.

David prized his retreat space, from the front door to the back of the yard, and I had to tip my hat to him, as he had put much of *his own intention* in bringing to its current state. He thanked me for my work, and told me that *even more importantly* than for his own benefit, he felt very thankful and privileged for the honor of helping two damaged souls navigate their way out of loss.

Intention

REALLY, THAT IS WHAT IT'S all about. For both the living *and* the dying, *intention* determines where we end up. My work is directing energy, with *intention,* and when I meet clients who want me not only to resolve a difficult situation in their home, but to help them manifest their own intention, I know that it's already done.

Fixing A Hole

Susan Van Horn was referred to me by a close friend, who was coaching her through some major life shifts. Emerging from a divorce, Susan was trying to stabilize the Bed & Breakfast she and her (now ex) husband had built, before it dragged her into bankruptcy. She had a very specific and uplifting intention to recreate the place as a retreat center, The Center for Soul, but was being opposed at every turn. Perhaps her intention brought us to that small degree of separation, for although my friend had never experienced my work, she trusted that I was the only option for Susan's life making or breaking situation.

Susan's life was a beehive, she was extremely involved in the upkeep of the building, running it as a B&B, its finances and securing a loan, the business plan, and of course, her children and their safety, *all at the same time.* She was quite concerned about one of the upstairs suites, which had been home to some unpleasantness, and recognized that the charge made it a much less pleasant guest room than it would ordinarily be.

She was concerned for her children's welfare, as well, as the transition had been difficult for them too. Susan mentioned to me that her daughters still refused to sleep in their room, and her concern over her their fears was part of the reason that she had contacted me. To heal the house was one job, to reformat it another, and to calm her family situation still another, but she offered to let me stay as a guest, so I figured I'd have time.

For being built in 1867, the structure itself was very large, and it had seen much in its transition from dilapidated farmhouse (with no electricity, running water, or indoor plumbing) to a beautiful seaside inn. It had fallen into great disrepair, being left to rot in its original location, and become home not only to the swallows, but to vagrants, who left it feeling not quite as a home should. A developer had seen it lying fallow in a field, purchased it for a pittance, and started a remodel project with his family. *That's when it started costing.* The project took years and his children lost interest. Susan and her husband had purchased it from him and moved it several miles to its present location, and then *their* troubles began.

The first thing about I noticed was that the house felt extremely cluttered, thick with old energy and negative emotion. Despite its *complete* rebuilding, the main staircase retained a spooky, off-kilter funkiness, and Susan commented on how some of the planned architectural updates were put off or let go due to challenges with the construction company. It seemed that the building's retained energy was *not permitting change*, on a grand scale, or lesser, for that matter. No longer on its original grounding or in compass alignment at all with its original foundation, it was holding on to its own death picture, and taking them with it.

While the area to which it had been moved was quite lovely, looking on to a large flower farm near the ocean, the crust of its hundred-year demise, and the very difficult years since they had purchased it, made it something of a job to simply align it with the earth energy there, and I had to start by creating an entirely new grounding for it.

Looking through the older layers, it appeared that the deaths that had occurred in the house were not particularly traumatic. They had come at a time when people birthed and died at home, and the attendant emotion from them was not so significant as to make for great difficulty. But the contractual sense that the house itself had died its own sort of death made it feel unfit to be a residence.

The business aspect flowed no more easily, and running it from an office there created a dualistic life for Susan, imbalancing her personal life against the professional tasks at hand. While the B&B required her focus, her focus required a grounded, settled place to work from, one that didn't bleed around the edges. So creating clear separations between the work of the place where she lived and the life that she was living there, was essential.

Moving into the upstairs, and the suite that held the dis-ease of her relationship demise, I could feel the emotional upset that still reverberated through the house. It was a job that called for sweeping changes of energy, moving columns of earth and light through the building. From a window there I was presented with a staggering view of the flower farm next door, and I tuned into that. Pulling the color and vibrancy of acres of sunlit flowers in bloom through the house, I washed and rinsed the stagnant energy of its history, dissolved the more present-time energy of Susan's family breakdown, and refreshed the suites so that guests, rather than being confronted by any foreign emotional burden, would only find rejuvenation in the delightful setting they were in.

Coming back down the stairs, which seemed noticeably safer, I moved into Susan's daughters' room. It had become - partly because of the divorce and the disparate energies of time-sharing with either parent - kind of a disaster area. Lovely decor, but so strewn with toys and dolls and stuffed animals that it lacked a comfortable place to settle down. It appeared to me that this room may have been the room where some deaths had occurred, as the energy there was quite stagnant, and probably due to some of the more recent emotional development, unrestful.

With their father no longer living there, and his visitation causing duress for their mother, it was necessary to make grounded emotional separations between both parents and their connections to the girls, who had become relational fulcrums. Susan's divorce created quite an upheaval for her daughters, and that energy needed to be abolished from their room. I thoroughly cleared and reset it for their greatest emotional grounding, so that they could live without that cloud of uncertainty.

Once the house was clear, I could look into the future plans Susan had for the center, envision the future remodeling, and get to work on the financial and business aspects that Susan required to move into a more prosperous, professional state. I slept quite well in the house that night, and when I met Susan in the morning she told me, astonished, that her daughters had slept in their own beds.

Crack House

Sharon had purchased a duplex along with a former client of mine, Ann, who, from the time of purchase, had realized that it would be a good house to have me work on. Ann was having some minor issues upstairs, but the lower unit, which Sharon had purchased, was severely problematic. The house was situated in a gentrifying North Oakland neighborhood, with a period paint job and completely new interiors, a beautiful kitchen, granite counters, bamboo floors; from all appearances, *perfect.*

But what they found after speaking with the neighbors, was that the house — which they knew had been stripped down to the beams, re-plumbed, rewired, and rebuilt from the ground up — had been a long-time crack house. It was "the house on the corner that everyone in the neighborhood feared, or frequented to purchase drugs." It had gotten to such a state that the cracklords had installed a cyclone fence around it, with the strip of yard patrolled by pit bulls. Entry was solely for those who had commerce to attend to.

Sharon complained to me about the inhospitable feeling of certain rooms and the peculiar contradiction in the house. As someone who likes to let in the light and look out on the world, she was attracted to the fact that it was wrapped with windows. But after she moved in, the windows began to feel oppressive to her, like they needed to be covered, or hidden from, and she, a very social person, needed to seclude herself there. There was a particularly problematic room that she had set aside as her office. It had a large closet with its own window at the end, which had initially attracted her and in which she had tried to create a meditation room, but it wasn't working. Nor was the office, which was still (two months after moving in) a pile of boxes, clutter, and uninstalled computer parts and peripherals.

Mind you, Sharon's décor and sensibilities were quite tasteful and well organized. She had spent some time in Japan and had a lot of Japanese artwork and living essentials. That sensibility, of sparing organization, definitely showed in her layout of the house, which was quite lovely. But the office was off-limits. And as for the meditation chamber, it was not a place to enter.

When I began to feel my way around the house, I was met with the sensation of being in a cage, or perhaps a fish tank, an incredible feeling of paranoid death wish, embedded by the crack house years. I don't know if you have ever smoked crack, but the sense I got from it was that people used this space to escape their lives, their loves, their responsibilities, commitments, families, children, pain, loss, anger, depression, escape everything. Despite the painful expense of their pursuit, the attraction to these moments of escape led a stream of people through these doors.

Chasing the flame to the land of ecstatic nothingness, while fearing being seen in their most undignified existential-grasping, left them naked and exposed. And waiting for the police to kick in the door and drag them back into the harsh light of their reality turned every sound, every shadow, every passing headlight into a heart pounding terror, and made the windows lenses to be hidden from. As the crack house years went on, its denizens' condemnation of the outside world, *and their lives as well,* created a vortex, a black hole whose gravity was inescapable for all who slipped over the event horizon.

The overlording energy of those who profiteered this social need for disengagement left a very unpleasant air, and the guest bedroom brought to mind the economics of human suffering. It appeared to be a room where women prostituted themselves to obtain their supply of crack. This cycle of degradation was played out on a daily basis between various parties as they sought their dissolution, and their pleasure from degrading those who could no longer afford their own vice. It was what I term a *"sick room,"* and it needed some definite change of energy.

The office too held some of this sickness, but also something deeper. As the most enclosed room (I think it was the manager's), it held an impossible-to-overcome sense of life gone awry, spent in the money-seeking, pleasure-seeking, life-rejecting, fearful hollow of crack dealing. Seeking escape from the reality of ghetto life through the money and power, one falls prey to the drug which brings them to you. It rips you away from your family, friends, and any human connection but the basest of the marketplace, creates the constant fear of the police, rivals, murder, and generally distorts your ego to a point of craven desperation.

The low point of the house, in something of the physical and certainly the psychological *bowels* of the office, lay the windowed closet. Now Sharon's beautifully appointed "meditation room," it had been the hidden, locking cell, where one could literally disappear and smoke crack into oblivion. The sense of seeking *and finding* oblivion was far more potent than all the bells and altars Sharon had arranged there in her search for enlightenment, and made it an impossible place to sit, seek clarity, or even breathe.

The bedroom that Sharon had chosen had a much more flowing energy, probably because it was originally the kitchen. It had quite a few windows on the street and opened into the side yard, so was less of a room that people could hide in while abusing themselves. It was an easier place for her to settle into (despite the windows) and the best place for me to start grounding the house. Fortunately, it had stood there for 70 years and could return to its previously grounded state once offered that choice. While the building hadn't asked for it, the contract for living had been shifted greatly during the crack house years, and despite its physical renewal it still stood as a fear-ravaged hideout.

Its contracts needed to be completely re-thought and re-written, as it was now intended to be a sanctuary; a place particularly focused on social contact, community, clarity, and spiritual growth. With that intention, there was no longer room for the oppressive, tormenting, self-negating energy that held sway, it only had to be *removed.*

Fortunately, Sharon's Japanese décor scheme worked well with my aesthetic, and after getting my bearings, I moved into her meditation chamber. Using every technique at my disposal, as well as the iconic tools on her altar, I finally hit a zero point and established clarity. Then, magnifying Sharon's singing bowl a thousand times, I began ringing a giant Japanese temple bell, vibrating away the death-seeking soul-selling pollution, and expanding a grounded, clarifying, light-filled temple energy throughout the entire flat. This was precisely the energy that Sharon had wanted to invite in, and after discharging the windows' conscription as fear-laden portholes to a threatening outside world, they became opportunities for light and air to continually refresh the premises.

Despite the outward renovations having been completed for over a year, the neighborhood's entrenched memory of a blighted and threatening crack house still remained. The one concession to life that had remained through it all was a tremendous bougainvillea out front, which, during the worst of it, had the tenacity to grow through the cyclone fence, inviting young and old to come by and have their picture taken in front of it. It had been pruned back but was still healthy, and using its energy to reset the visage of the house, while dissolving the neighbors' outdated expectations, ushered in a new era.

I left that job feeling very positive about the work done for my client, the house, and the outward community. I hope that I helped Sharon establish a place for community, in the place where those neighbors lost so much.

Part III

House Healing Around The World

IN 1996 THE SAN FRANCISCO *Examiner* interviewed me for an article in their HOME section. I told the reporter that the best way for her to understand my work would be for me to clean her house. She demurred, replying that there were no problems there. I told here she didn't need a ghost to feel the effect of my work, that it was all about her relationship to the house, and that she really couldn't understand it from an outside "objective" standpoint.

Still, that was too much to ask (or offer), so we went along with the usual interview process, which led to a rational, mildly skeptical article.

I spoke with her a few months after it ran, and apparently, talking to my clients had got her thinking. She admitted to me that she had always hated her kitchen, and that from the time they had purchased their house, her husband had promised to remodel it.

Ten years had gone by and she was still hating it. But in the month after writing the article, her kitchen had suffered an electrical fire, which was finally getting her the remodel she had always wanted. I told her that it might have been easier to let me clean the house, but you get what you ask for.

After the article ran I received a call from a Hindu man that went something like this. "Are you the man from the article, who cleans spirits out of houses?"

"Yes, that's me."

"Then you are of the Brahmin class, and I would like to invite you to our temple."

"Well, I've always liked to think of myself in that light, I'd be most honored."

"Are you familiar with the different rituals of *puja?*"

"No, I've never heard the word."

"Hmm. In our culture, we perform a cleansing whenever a building is built, or someone moves into it. For example, a newly married couple would have a puja for their new home."

"Wow! I had no idea. I'd love to come."

"Are you a vegetarian?"

"Well, I was for many years, but my Chinese doctor has me eating beef again."

"No."

"Yeah."

"Then you cannot come to our temple."

"Ohhhh, man. I won't eat any meat that week."

"No, no, that won't do, I am so sorry."

"Mmm, me too."

That was when I realized that Healing Houses is truly a multicultural affair. As my studies of Chinese Medicine progressed, I delved into Feng Shui, which was already the rage in the Bay Area, and got a pretty good education in it. Enough to consider that my Hindu caller may have been right, that except for my carnivorous spiritual failings, I was working at a certain level of distinction.

Everywhere But Here

Over the years, I've looked into a variety of traditions, many of which my clients tried before calling me. Native American smudging, arcane Wicca blessings, Feng Shui and its ubiquitous mirrors, all tell of people attempting to live in harmony with their homes. My editor even told me of a Catholic exorcism performed for her immigrant grandparents in New Jersey. It appears that the interface between our living space and the energetic realm is well respected in cultures that have a culture, so I've taken some time to document some of these practices as a means of putting my own in context.

Puja – India

The Hindus have long been known as the most religious culture in the world, rife with observance and celebration. *Puja*, a ritual performed to show respect to the gods, precedes many special occasions, and is part of the traditional house warming.

Puja consists of dozens of prescribed steps, depending on sect or family tradition. These always include forms of meditation, austerity, chanting, scriptural reading, food offering, and prostrations. Puja may be performed by an individual worshipper or in gatherings. The ritual may be observed in silence or accompanied by prayers. Sometimes a puja is done for the benefit of certain people, for whom priests or relatives ask blessings.

Pujas are not performed as rites intended to clear a house after someone's death, that task is essentially ingrained into the culture. While the mortal remains are quickly dispatched (by pyre or by being floated down the holy river, with proper rites performed, of course), traditionally, all of the deceased's belongings, clothing, furniture, and personal items are given away, particularly the deathbed itself, which goes first to the family butler (in a middle class family), or in a village, may be set outside the house.

Whether that bed or any other articles contain a sliver of the deceased's karmic remnants I rather doubt, as India is the home of reincarnation. Accepting this philosophy (which current research substantiates), people are attuned to the concept that death is simply a movement toward a different *life,* which they are prone to greeting.

I very much respect this concept, and would have been most glad to attend ceremonies at the Hindu temple to which I was invited. Unfortunately, my respect for my Chinese doctor's dietary recommendations left me out in the cold, *for this lifetime.*

Feng Shui – China

Feng Shui is an ancient Taoist science developed to create a harmonious connection between people and their living/work space. It was originally developed to help ensure proper grave site placement for the royal family. In a culture that has always stressed honoring one's ancestors, this is an important decision. Eventually Feng Shui evolved into a system of designing the architecture of the king's palace, to optimize his health and rulership, and moved beyond that into the design of the imperial city. The ancient Taoists had an eye for the patterns of the world, how they affect all of us, and how to interact with these patterns in a healthful way. From the same philosophical observations of nature came the interrelated systems of Chinese medicine, the Chinese calendar, and Ba Zi (a divination method based on earth's angular alignment with the sun).

Feng Shui (pronounced fung shway) has been in use for thousands of years to create a stronger connection to the building site, enhance defense, create tranquility, and promote health and prosperity. The location of a building, its position on a site, the architectural elements and interior layout all have effects on the mental state, health, productivity and prosperity of the workers and the business itself. This is why more modern businesses are taking a tip from the east, and trying to enhance the Feng Shui of their offices; good design pays for itself.

Much of Feng Shui deals with what is called "enhancement." This is the modification of elements of a building to promote positive energy flow. Since Feng Shui looks at spaces as being eight-sided (with ⅜ths positively and ⅜ths *negatively* aspected — *and a quarter neutral*), correct enhancement is essential. Enhancements can be based in the architectural, landscape, or interior design of a building, but much of what we see in the West as Feng Shui has been simplified to the point of losing its scientific core.

The simple eight directional layout referred to as the Ba Gua is actually much more complex. Denoting the positive and negative areas of a structure, it has eight different arrangements, depending on the direction the building faces. The enhancements to be made to the space must be based on the personal ba gua of the person living there, which again may be one of eight different layouts, and runs clockwise or counter clock-wise depending on their sex. This creates over a hundred different possible enhancements for any one area for any particular person. A knowledge of Ba Zi is also essential for determining a client's elemental constitution before advising them on physical environment, as the wrong enhancement can seriously affect the health of the client. While a simple approach to harmonious design principles is nice, real Feng Shui is a complicated subject.

While I have a solid working knowledge of Feng Shui, I have been solicited by my Chinese clients for my ability to work at the subtle levels that most practitioners are not aware of. Feng Shui itself is very useful for designing space or correcting problems in chi flow. It does not, however, remove imbedded energies. Good Feng Shui will make it more difficult for bad chi to accumulate, but serious Feng Shui texts state that removal of a ghost requires the services of a priest.

Call me what you want, just call me.

Wicca

Far from being a bizarre cult (as it has been painted by the brush of ignorance), Wicca reflects the true Pagan cultural heritage of northern Europe. As a nature worship system, Paganism honors the concrete manifestations of our physical world, the four directions and the elements that they beget, earth, air, fire and water, the earth itself, the sky and stars, sun and moon, all the different life forms with which we co-exist and interdepend, and the gods and goddesses who lend personas to the archetypes.

Similarly to my own practice, Wicca house clearing uses three formats, cleansing, banishment, and protection. Cleansing would be used in general circumstances, i.e. a new house blessing, whereas banishment would deal specifically with an invasive energy that was bothering the inhabitants. Protection might be set after either, or done as a stand alone ritual.

In any Wicca ritual, a circle is cast, which acknowledges the directions, and opens the ritual space to their healing energies, whereupon whichever god/ess is invoked to lend their aid. Upon learning of the particular problem a house has, the practitioner will determine which god(ess)'s domain(s) includes that issue, and how to best invoke them.

Once the circle is open, the practitioner(s) will start in the doorway, and move around the house, dousing it with salt water, burning sage, and ringing bells, or using whatever magic items they prefer to cleanse and purify. A second round is made, sweeping good energy *in* with a special broom (the witch's broom). In Banishment rituals, the practitioners will move around the house in a counterclockwise direction, or *Widdershins,* which is used to drive out energy (albeit with the intention that spirits will move toward love and light). Cleansing and Protection rituals are conducted clockwise, or *Deosil*, with the intention of bringing in all the good things for life, or setting up defenses against negative influences.

For protection, the practitioner may leave amulets, stones, herbs, or ward-offs, such as the *Eye of Horus*, the *Hand of Fatima*, or handcrafted items charged with protective spells. Often a candle is wrapped in paper, upon which is written a list of all the positive qualities the resident wishes to bring into their home. The candle is burned during the ceremony, then extinguished, and given to the resident to light again when they feel the need to bring those things back into their home.

Exorcism

From the earliest days of my work, my friends have giddily called me "the Exorcist," and I must admit to occasionally (as I approach a client's home) envisioning myself in that famous shot of Max von Sydow, standing in the lamplight in front of Linda Blair's house. In some respects, we're in the same business, although I like to think I have a broader perspective. As my editor described it though, the exorcism of her grandparents' house was somewhat akin to a Hindu puja or pagan ritual. The priest came and sprinkled holy water in all the corners, and perhaps salt as well. Candles were burned and prayers were read to cast out the spirits. Not as personal as my work, but following in a long tradition.

According to my research on Catholic belief, *demons* or *fallen angels* retain their natural ability to act on the material universe, using material objects and directing material forces for their own "*wicked*" ends. While this power is subject (of course) to the control of divine providence, said *demons are* believed to have been allowed a wide scope for their activity as a consequence of the sin of mankind. Hence *places and things* as well as persons are naturally liable to diabolical infestation, within limits permitted by said "god."

The actual format of exorcism was revised quite recently. Replacing one which was promulgated as part of the Roman Ritual of 1614, *De Exorcismus et supplicationibus quibusdam* was approved by Pope John Paul II on October 1, 1998. The document set out a new and precise liturgical form for the rite of exorcism, entirely in Latin. In a short introduction, the document calls attention to the existence of both *"angelic creatures"* and others *"called demons, who are opposed to God."* Since the influence of the demonic can become apparent in people, *places,* or things, the document continues, the Church "has prayed, and continues to pray, that men will be freed from the snares of the Devil."

Used mostly on individuals, the liturgical ritual itself is centered on prayers of supplication, asking for God's help, and "imperative" prayers addressed directly to the Devil, commanding him to depart. The prayers are to be said as the exorcist lays his hand on the individual, and are part of an overall ritual which includes specific blessings and sprinklings with holy water.

Making Your Home Your Own

A Caveat

WHEN I BEGAN THINKING ABOUT this book, I had no intention of using it as a teaching device, in terms of actually doing the work I do. In fact, I specifically stated that it would *not* be a "How To" book. With some prodding, however, I came to realize that my readers won't all be able (or really need) to enlist my services, and that addressing what they can do on their own would be valuable for them. That said, I must state clearly: If your home holds a serious energy problem, attempting to take it on without thorough training can cause illness, and make the problem worse.

I consider what I do to be serious professional work, for which I have trained and developed my capacity over many years, and in most unlikely ways. Almost entirely, these have been through personal experience. While books are fantastic information sources, the part of your brain that is used while reading is not that which is used in *meditating*. This is why meditation is best taught by a teacher who can lead you into focusing your mind, and help you learn to direct it yourself.

Learning The Work

After I had developed my practice for several years, I realized it would be a good thing to teach as a graduate seminar at the

Academy. While serious house problems are not the norm, most sensitive people feel their house could use some work, so I had pretty good turnout. Respecting my skill as a teacher, and the value of the subject, the registrar suggested that I open the class to general enrollment.

I was concerned about this for a couple of reasons. First off, I wanted to be sure that anyone engaging in this work had a solid capacity for grounding, setting protection, and clearing their own energy system. You can never tell what's going on with a house until you're in it, and without being able to hold your own, you could get thrown into a tailspin.

What I realized about the classroom setting, however, was that everyone would be distanced from their homes, which would make it much safer for them. While some students were querulous over working remotely, I knew that they knew their homes well enough to visualize them and feel their energy, simply from memory. In my first open class, a physics professor from University of California attended with his wife. Bob was probably my greatest skeptical challenge, but he got through the meditations well, and emailed me the next week to tell me that his house felt distinctly different.

Working remotely gives my students the chance to directly experience their perceptual capacity, *and* investigate their home's energy without directly engaging it. Assuming you've subscribed to your home's contracts, or have developed some relationship to an energetic presence there, doing this work will also affect you personally, which can be quite disorienting. It's like moving the rug while you're standing on it, *except that it's actually moving.* Without a solid grounding, good protection, and clear perception, clearing is very difficult, and those are the first things to go when you're merged with another energy. In ancestral homes, one's own memories or connections to now deceased loved ones can make doing it impossible.

Obviously, if you have a serious problem, I'd like you call me, but if that's not the case, and you can't attend one of my workshops, there are definitely things you *can* do to improve the feel of your home, from an energetic level.

The Importance of Intention

"Energy follows your thought," so it's imperative to visualize the details of your home as you would ultimately like it to be, with particular attention to what it would *feel* like. *Where would you like to be living, geographically?* In a forest, by the ocean, or perhaps in the desert? The environmental setting has a lot to do with how you will feel, and perhaps with directing what you're moving toward. *What kind of property would it be?* Is it a Zendo, or a nightclub, or a ranch house, or something in between? *What level of vibrancy or tranquility feels most comfortable to you? What kind of structure would it be?* A geodesic dome, with glass walls, or a cave dwelling? Don't let the current physical structure limit your visualization of what it could be or *feel* like.

Who lives with you, and who is not allowed to visit? Our families and friends play an important role in our lives, but they can overwhelm our energy as well. Some people want their children's house to be the neighborhood playground, some would pull their hair out. Set your intention and make it so. *Do you work at home?* Envision a separated office area, so you can keep work productive *and* leave it behind. Make a list of the attributes and accents that you'd like your house to house to have, and spend some time visualizing how they would overlay your house as it stands.

Make Offerings

Assuming that you are a lay reader, I'd rather not have you attempt any practices that would challenge any energies beyond your capacity. Even smudging, I have heard, can aggravate things when not undertaken by someone with the authority to use it properly. In all traditions, however, approaching unknowns with respect and honoring their situation can only be seen as positive.

You may not feel comfortable (or sane) trying to engage your house in a dialogue about its history and health, although you might accept that what you feel about it is true to some degree. Trust your intuition. You live there. If you can sit quietly and focus on where the house feels uncomfortable, and *how* it feels exactly, you can probably ascertain some clue as to what's going on. It's never so important to me to know the exact details, as much as to be aware of the energy and shift it.

Ask the house itself to accept you as the new tenant/owner, and to bring itself into alignment with the earth on this calendar day. (Leaving the past behind is a major ordeal for most of us, but a house knows of nothing else.) Assuming you have a sense of what's *off* energetically, ask the house to release it into the earth, and make a mental commitment to be disengaged from it yourself. If you feel there is a specific spirit, ask it to be healed and complete its journey.

When you've looked into the various situations, and asked for their release and renewal, make offerings to the house and to the energies you've asked to leave it. Light candles, place flowers, plants, fruit, oils, crystals, water, or whatever objects you deem appropriate in the affected rooms. Open the windows and ask the house to breathe in a new day.

Rituals for Renewal

Almost no one in our culture makes any acknowledgment of the tremendous life shift that occurs when moving. It's just *order a pizza and wait for the cable guy.* What I tell my clients when I'm done working on a house is to make up their own ritual for taking ownership, which is a good idea for *anyone* who moves into a new place.

I place no limitations on what a ritual might be, but note that it should include the entire family, and preferably, fun. Clearly, some sort of prayer is a good start, an acknowledgement of the four directions and whatever spirit helpers you ascribe to. After that, any activity that carries your life essence (making art, reading poetry, planting flowers, cooking a fabulous meal, having sex, *playing ping-pong, having sex while playing ping-pong!), anything* that you can ritualize for this purpose, do! Be sure to add music; drums, rattles, gongs, bells, whistles, brass bands, kazoos, geetars, or a gentle piano, singing, humming, chanting, or yodeling, and always always, always, dancing, and you should be in good stead.

Affirmations for Your Home

You may find it helpful to place affirmations around your home, to remind you of the energy setting you are consciously creating. A hand-written note under a fridge magnet or a post-it on your desk or dresser will occasionally invite you to re-vision your intentional picture of how your house should feel.

My home shelters me from the world.
My home is calm, relaxed, and joyous.
My home is a place for my family to be together.
My home invites tranquility.
My home makes everyone feel welcome.
My home allows me to be centered.
My home is fun!
My home lets me connect to nature.
My home is a place where love flourishes.
My home is a place for (whatever is most important to you).

Reflections

It's been a long process, coming to this work, *and to this book,* and I've introduced plenty of stumbling blocks along the way. Even now, sitting in my office, it's still a little hard to believe. So if you're skeptical, be not ashamed. I am, most of the time. It's safer, and easier. It's important to recognize, however, the difference between *critical,* and *discerning,* and always to pay attention to how things *feel.*

As Ba Zi suggests, we all have greatly varying elemental composition, which belie our mental/emotional framework. Some people are more open, sensitive to energy, a sense of wonder, and spiritual connection. Some are more hardened, and sarcastic. Oddly, I'm both. But within us all is the yearning, for connection, clarity, and peace of mind.

New Physics

While it's easy to find proclamations that modern science does *not* support the existence of ghosts, or any such phenomena, there is no evidence to prove it. In fact, current models of quantum physics indicate that our physical bodies are actually vibrational interference between atoms, that our minds are not directly connected to our bodies, that our hearts and organs send and receive waveform information and that our thoughts themselves interact with the physical world through such things as the "Observer Effect." While some refuse to consider that there is more to the world than what is mediated by our five senses, scientists have determined that there are at least 19 discreet senses, and as sensitivity to bio-energetic transmission is being lab tested, probably more.

While scarcely heard of in the mainstream press, The Institute of Noetic Sciences backs a broad array of hard scientific research on such topics as Non-locality of Consciousness, and the Human Bio-field and its implications in healing, among other things. They have published a number of double-blind, controlled studies that clearly indicate that our bodies know more than we do, and that our minds do much more than we think.

Laser inventing physicist Russel Targ's lab at the Stanford Research Institute was drafted by the CIA in the mid-seventies, to developed a number of highly skilled remote viewers, whose skills they applied not only to looking at specific physical sites, but at future probabilities. If the government is hiring people to look into the future, why are we stuck watching television?

Famed neurosurgeon Dr. Norman Shealey's pioneering work on energy healing has opened the whole field of medical intuition, while supporting the development of *therapeutic touch* in hospitals where it is most needed. Still, most of us are waiting in line for health insurance, or if we can afford it, at the pharmacy, for a pill to take away the way we *feel*.

As more credible research into the physics and biophysics of psi is conducted, there is more for us to wrap our minds around. It's a precipice, no doubt, to leave the Cartesian/Newtonian framework behind and pay attention to the underlying substrate of reality is not for everyone. There is plenty of evidence, however, for those who desire scientific substantiation for what their experience has already told them.

On Personal Work

Occasionally I am asked to do the work I trained in, and it's said that I'm no slouch. At the time I was getting into it though, I had some personal issues of my own to work out, and didn't feel as comfortable as I do now in asking people to expose themselves to my x-ray vision, or to discuss their personal issues. Maybe it was just a guy thing, and I didn't expect my guy friends to be into talking about emotional stuff either. As I got more intent on house work though, I became attracted to certain facets of it which differ from working on people.

Houses have no expectations or self-imposed limitations. The work may be difficult, tragic, gnarly and weird, but the objective is always the zero point. I like to get my job done in one shot, which may take several hours, but I do it. Facilitating healing in people is a long, involved process, for which, ultimately, the client must assume responsibility. Raised with our Western medical model, we expect our practitioners to heal us, and personal healing on the energetic level requires tremendous, and often uncomfortable, change.

As was pointed out to me by my Chinese medicine teacher, I *can not* ***heal*** a person, particularly in one or even a few sessions. Change must be made gradually, from within, through realization and alteration in behavior, with, of course, assistance of a facilitator when asked for. It's not particularly disempowering for me to recognize that fact, but I do like to work at my highest capacity and effect concrete change.

While I've learned to use compassion and tact in dealing with the departed, I feel free to use all the tools at my disposal when working on a house, in order to get the job done. It's a dude thing, and my clients appreciate it. It's not asking too much of them, and it gets the results they want.

Asking clients to join me in my rather rigorous healing

protocol, which includes hypnotherapy and Chinese organ massage, is a little more demanding, so for the most part, I'm happy just to give them a place to live. If you're interested in personal work, however, you can reach me through my website.

Hire Me?

As much as I want this book to be a general reference work, it's going to pertain more to some people than others. If you're reading it because your home has a situation resembling one of those I've described, *even weirder*, or simply does not feel like your own, I am at your service.

It usually takes me about a half day to do a house, although size and nature of problem can add to that. Some clients like to be home while I'm there, others prefer to leave. (I'm sure either feels a little odd.) As long as I have a quiet place to meditate, I'm fine, although it's good for me to be able to walk through the house with them initially.

If you're interested in having me work for you, go to my website — *www.HealingHouses.com* — where you'll find my questionnaire. If you want me to work on your business, you'll find a separate form.

No matter what shape your house is in, if you've read this book, you may want to answer my questionnaire, just so you know your own home better.

Questionnaire

1. What are the full names of all family members/residents/pets?
2. Who were the original owners and previous tenants?
3. Was there a death, long term illness, divorce or other family trauma in the house?
4. Do you have any particular sensations or feelings in the house? In certain rooms? From furniture?
5. Have you had any occurrence or suspicion of ghostly activity?
6. Is there any personal history or events I should know about?
7. How are your neighbor relations? Any bad ones?
8. What is the age and history of the house?
9. Has it ever suffered damages or disasters?
10. Are you considering selling the house? Price?
11. Where would you ideally like to be living?
12. How would you ultimately like your house to feel?

More Caveats – Front to Back

I'll admit, there are things I usually don't tell my clients until the time is right. It's weird enough being in this business, and I want my clients to relax and know that things are in hand. If you've read this far, and you're thinking about having me work on your house, you can probably deal with them.

Up Front – *They know I'm coming.* I don't know how (okay, maybe I know how), but problematic spirits seem to respond to the fact that my clients have set up an appointment with me. Acting on your intention to own your space puts them on the defensive, and their response is usually to turn things up a notch. No one wants that, which is why I usually don't tell my clients until we've set a date. Before this book, it only took a week or two to get an appointment, so it was never too much of a problem. Now, I'm not sure, but your options are clear — you can go on living in *their* home, or not.

In the Middle – Occasionally I see things, in the midst of the work, that relate to my clients. While I'm not intentionally doing a personal reading for you, your energy is *all over the place,* and as I clean your closets, *literally and figuratively,* I may bump up against your stuff. Please don't be offended if I have to ask a question or two about how certain charges relate to you.

On the Back End – Some of my clients find that they have a new problem to deal with when I'm gone — What to do with all that space? When you're no longer fighting against patterns that don't belong to you, it's like suddenly being able to breathe again, and when you empty a room of all it's stale energy, there's suddenly room for all of yours. This can be tremendously liberating — or somewhat daunting.

What I tell my clients is to be prepared to feel their own feelings, which could result in a period of relationship adjustment, as they deal with the *unaffected* sense of their own family dynamics. For some, this means dealing with issues that have been brewing on the back burner, and while that may be fear inducing, with a clear grounded space to communicate, it's certain to be transformative.

~Breathe~

About the Author

Sheldon Norberg, B.A. *(Psycho-Spiritual Healing)*, CMT, CHT

BEGINNING WITH TRANSCENDENTAL MEDITATION AT the age of ten, Sheldon Norberg's lifelong interest in states of consciousness led to a number of studies that helped organize his professional practice. After completing his Master of Intuition Medicine training at the Academy of Intuition Medicine®, he earned his BA in ***Psycho-Spiritual Healing*** (a program of his own design) at San Francisco State University.

He is certified both as a Chi Nei Tsang massage practitioner and Hypnotherapist, and has studied Holotropic Breathwork® with Stanislav Grof, Alchemical Divination with Ralph Metzner, and shamanism with Jose and Lena Stevens. He pulls from all these studies in his client work, although working with houses, offices, and other charged buildings is his greatest focus. Sheldon and his family live in Northern California.

Workshop Info

HAVING DESIGNED AND TAUGHT BASIC and advanced classes in this work at the Academy of Intuition Medicine®, I'm excited about the prospect of teaching workshops to the general public.

In these workshops you'll learn meditations to optimize the energetic structure of your home or office, and safely clear whatever prevents you from being completely grounded, protected and prosperous in your own space.

If you work with a bookstore, a community, spiritual, or retreat center, a psychotherapy or massage school, or some other suitable location, I offer day-long or weekend workshops for groups of 12-24 or more.

Go to **www.HealingHouses.com** for more information.

CPSIA information can be obtained at www.ICGtesting.com
Printed in the USA
LVOW11s1050100315

429928LV00004B/24/P